millennium

An Interdisciplinary Investigation

Daniel J. Barnekow

J. WESTON
WALCH
PUBLISHER
Portland, Maine

User's Guide
to
Walch Reproducible Books

As part of our general effort to provide educational materials which are as practical and economical as possible, we have designated this publication a "reproducible book." The designation means that purchase of the book includes purchase of the right to limited reproduction of all pages on which this symbol appears:

Here is the basic Walch policy: We grant to individual purchasers of this book the right to make sufficient copies of reproducible pages for use by all students of a single teacher. This permission is limited to a single teacher, and does not apply to entire schools or school systems, so institutions purchasing the book should pass the permission on to a single teacher. Copying of the book or its parts for resale is prohibited.

Any questions regarding this policy or requests to purchase further reproduction rights should be addressed to:

Permissions Editor
J. Weston Walch, Publisher
321 Valley Street • P. O. Box 658
Portland, Maine 04104-0658

1 2 3 4 5 6 7 8 9 10

ISBN 0-8251-2908-7

Contents

Unit II. The Millennium That Was

Unit III. An Event of a Lifetime: The Millennium Turns

Unit IV. The Millennium That Will Be: The 21st Century and Beyond

Preface

As we approach the turn of the millennium, more and more of what we read and hear starts with the phrase, "As we approach the turn of the millennium . . . ."

Why all the fuss? The answer may be that the turn of the millennium provides the same thrill as watching your car's odometer turn over at 100,000 miles—or happening to see the hour, minute, and second change all at once on a digital clock. The turn of the millennium gives us a chance to see something that usually seems to move at a glacial pace—history—actually progress.

The turn of the millennium marks the arrival of the ultimate benchmark date. When we were young, many of us calculated how old we would be in the year 2000. We grew up with television shows and magazine articles that promised "In the year 2000 . . ." life will be this, that, or the other—but always techno-exotic. Even centuries ago, forecasters chose 2000 as their benchmark date.

Of course, the millennium holds a greater significance for those Christians who view it as a time of peril and/or promise. Historians see it as a unique opportunity to evaluate the past 1,000 years. Observers of the human condition—philosophers, social scientists, artists, pundits, and the like—are keen to see how people react to the turn of the millennium.

Businesspeople naturally see in the turn of the millennium a once-in-a-thousand-years marketing opportunity. They are exploiting it much as they have exploited such events as the Bicentennial of the United States, the Quincentennial of Columbus's first voyage, and other major celebrations like the Olympic Games.

For these and other reasons, the turn of the millennium is very much a part of our zeitgeist. A slew of books, television shows, government reports, sermons, rock songs, and consumer goods named for, or marketed in the name of, the millennium are testaments to the hold the millennium has on the popular imagination.

This millennial awareness is, naturally, reaching children. For them, the turn of the millennium will remain an outstanding memory for the rest of their lives. The purpose of this book is to give them—and you—a framework to view this lifetime event in a thoughtful way. By examining the turn of the millennium through the lenses of various disciplines, young people can view and remember the event in something better than a pop fashion, and can learn vital, lasting lessons along the way. This is my hope, and I wish you success in communicating these more enduring messages to your students.

My hope is shared by the many people who have contributed significantly, and in various ways, to the creation of this book. Topping the list are the teachers and students who gave me invaluable advice as I created the lessons and activity sheets. They have my gratitude, as does Lisa French, for her support. Ken Kesner and Cynthia Hannon made important contributions. Still, I reserve my greatest appreciation for my daughter Kate, who has just informed me that she will be 8 years old in the year 2000.

—Dan Barnekow

To the Teacher

Millennium: An Interdisciplinary Investigation was written with the busy teacher in mind.

Throughout, lessons have been developed with input from students and experienced teachers. Each lesson has been field-tested when possible, or, at the very least, modeled on lesson formats that have proven results.

Millennium provides step-by-step teaching plans for each lesson and student activity sheet. Lesson objectives are clearly identified. Each lesson also includes extension and enrichment ideas; methods for formal, informal, and self-assessment; and student journal topics. The student activity sheets are written to meet your need of providing material for students of differing abilities and with different learning styles. There are individual, partner, and group activities; worksheet and hands-on activities; and activities that address the range of learning styles. Critical thinking skills are integrated throughout.

How the Book Is Organized

Millennium is organized into four units. Each unit comprises several lessons, with at least one student activity sheet for each lesson.

Unit I, "Once in a Thousand Years: The Turn of the Millennium," introduces students to the basic concepts necessary to study the turn of the millennium while accessing—and assessing, for you—their prior knowledge. Students explore the turn of the millennium through associated vocabulary, with time measurements, in the context of the Gregorian calendar, and as a salient, newsworthy event. They prepare a personalized plan of study and organize their learning in various formats.

Unit II, "The Millennium That Was," focuses students' attention on the second millennium. They complete various activities to appreciate the length of this era and the dramatic changes that occurred during it. They compare and contrast life in A.D. 1000 and A.D. 2000, and compare and contrast people's reactions to the first turn of the millennium and the second. A lighthearted lesson on what people have predicted the world would be like at the end of the second millennium closes the unit and prepares students to focus on the actual turn of the millennium.

Unit III, "An Event of a Lifetime: The Millennium Turns," is in many ways the heart of the book. Students perform computer searches and scavenger hunts to assess the societal attention being given the turn of the millennium. They also conduct interviews to better understand individuals' reactions to the event. Students calculate the date that the millennium will actually turn, and investigate how the turn will impact computers worldwide. Students reflect on leading thinkers' views on the meaning of the turn of the millennium, and on the art and special events that will celebrate and commemorate the event. They also investigate how the event has spawned a multibillion-dollar industry.

Unit IV, "The Millennium That Will Be: The 21st Century and Beyond," challenges students to think about the opening—and closing—of the next millennium. Students investigate the language challenges presented by the beginning of the new millennium, and create a time capsule for the people alive at the ending of the third millennium. The unit and book conclude with an opportunity for students to share whatever personal thoughts and feelings they care to about what they have studied.

Coverage of Disciplines

Millennium is an interdisciplinary book. The emphasis is on social studies, for the turn of the millennium is largely a social event. However, this unique event provides a unique opportunity for students to apply the tools of other disciplines to investigate a real-world happening. These disciplines include science, mathematics, computer science, art, and language arts.

Instructional Techniques

Millennium was created with a wide variety of teaching strategies and learning styles in mind.

Critical Thinking The percentage of critical thinking questions and activities in *Millennium* is extremely high. The very nature of the turn of the millennium almost requires such higher-order thinking skills to learn about it. Moreover, learning such skills is vital to young people. Every single lesson and every single activity sheet integrates critical thinking. The critical thinking skills emphasized are *interpretation, application, analysis, synthesis,* and *evaluation.*

Cooperative Learning Virtually every lesson in *Millennium* provides students with cooperative-learning opportunities. With a partner, within small groups, and as members of larger groups, students do much of their work as members of a team.

Traditional Learning Traditional learning techniques, in which students individually encounter and analyze a wide variety of material, are emphasized for the simple fact that they are irreplaceable.

Learning Styles The various ways that students learn are taken into account in both the activity sheets and the lesson plans. You will find some way to appeal to virtually all of your students within these pages. From reading aloud to reading maps, from oral reports to building models, from programming a computer to interviewing a relative, all types of learners' interests and abilities are accommodated.

Ability Levels Students are of different learning abilities, and so the activity sheets in *Millennium* are designed for and designated at three levels. These designations are:

A: easy
B: intermediate
C: advanced

The designation of each activity sheet is specified in the lesson plan.

How to Use This Book

Millennium is designed to be extremely flexible. You could conceivably work from front to back, teaching every lesson and having students complete every activity sheet. Realistically, none of us has the time to devote to such an exhaustive study.

Therefore, the best approach may be for you to simply peruse the table of contents and the contents themselves, selecting lessons and activity sheets to tailor a program for your individual classes and students. For a brief, one-week course of study, consider assigning students the following activity sheets in the following order:

<u>Millennium: Short Program</u>
Student Activity Sheet 1A
Student Activity Sheet 4A
Student Activity Sheet 6A
Student Activity Sheet 12B
Student Activity Sheet 14B

By completing these activity sheets in the order specified, students will learn most of the essentials about the turn of the millennium.

Once in a Thousand Years:

THE TURN OF THE MILLENNIUM

LESSON 1: **The Turn of the Millennium**

Student Activity Sheet Disciplines and Levels

Student Activity Sheet	Discipline(s)	Level(s)
1A	social studies; language arts	A, B, C
1B	social studies	A, B, C
1C	social studies	A, B, C

Lesson Snapshot

As preparatory homework, students read and individually respond to a brief essay that introduces them to the concept of a millennium and to the essential fact that the millennium is about to turn. As in-class activities, students brainstorm with partners to assess their current knowledge about the turn of the millennium. As a follow-up lesson, they formulate questions they want answered about the turn of the millennium and propose ways they can find the answers to their questions.

Objectives

- Students will add *millennium* to their vocabulary and develop a context for learning about the turn of the millennium.

- Students will assess their current knowledge about the turn of the millennium.

- Students will formulate questions about the turn of the millennium.

- Students will propose ways to find out the answers to their questions about the turn of the millennium.

- Students will apply the following critical thinking skills: interpretation, analysis, synthesis, and evaluation.

Class Time Required

- 1 class period

Materials Needed

- Student Activity Sheets 1A, 1B, and 1C
- pencils or pens

Lesson Plan

1. PREPARE

Before class you should . . .

- review the lesson materials;
- consider which students you would like to work together as partners.

Before class students should . . .

- complete Student Activity Sheet 1A as preparatory homework.

2. TEACH

Focus

- Launch the lesson by writing *millennium* on the chalkboard and challenging volunteers to explain its significance.

- Guide students into identifying *millennium* as both a time period (any 1,000 years can be called a millennium) and as any logical grouping of 1,000 years.

- Ask students why the concept of a millennium has special significance during their own lifetimes.

Guide

- Organize the class into partners.

- Distribute one copy of Student Activity Sheet 1B to each student and instruct them to complete it. Direct pairs of students to work together, but to complete their own activity sheets as they work.

- Allow time for the partners to complete their task. As the students work, circulate to keep them on track. Pay attention to particular students' attitudes and contributions. Encourage students to list anything relevant, no matter how seemingly insignificant, in their charts. Encourage students to encourage each other.

Close

- Once students have completed their tasks, release them to their individual desks.

- As a class-discussion activity, create a "What We Know About the Turn of the Millennium" chart on the chalkboard by having students volunteer information from their activity sheets.

- Add a second column to the class chart, and label it "Questions We Have About the Turn of the Millennium." Challenge students to identify as many questions as they can, and record them on the chart.

- Conclude by distributing Student Activity Sheet 1C as an individual homework assign-ment. Emphasize that long lists in the questions demonstrate curiosity and expansive thinking, and not ignorance. You might want to stimulate thinking for the question column by having students think about the basic questions—who, what, where, when, why, and how—as they apply to the turn of the millennium.

3. EVALUATE

- **Formal Evaluation** Collect and examine individual students' work on Student Activity Sheets 1A and 1C.

- **Informal Evaluation** Observe individual students' attitudes and contributions during the partner work period.

- **Self-Evaluation** Have students consider these questions: Did I know more or less than I thought I knew? How will this activity help me learn more, and more efficiently, in the future?

4. EXTENSION AND ENRICHMENT

- Encourage students to use similar charts in other subjects and for other assignments.

- Create and maintain the class-wide versions of charts created for this lesson.

- Have students keep a log in which they record the answers to their questions and explain how they found the answers.

Teacher to Teacher: The best part of this activity is the class chart. It really helps the students appreciate the fact that they are all in the same boat, and it promotes team spirit. It really helps me, because it's an excellent way to assess prior knowledge and to plan my teaching to get the greatest results.

Journal Activities

You may wish to assign the self-evaluation questions as journal topics. As an alternative, challenge students to explore further this question: Where did I learn what I already knew about the millennium?

Once in a Thousand Years

You will soon witness one of the rarest events in human history—an event that occurs, literally, only once in a thousand years. Do you know what it is? Will you be ready for it?

Focus | Read the following essay. Then answer the questions about the essay.

Millennium: Once in a Thousand Years

Memorize this word: *millennium* (muh LEN ee um). If you haven't heard it yet, you soon will. And there's a good chance you will hear it nearly every day until the year 2001, and beyond. Why? Because the millennium is about to change, and this change will be one of the most important and talked-about events of your entire life.

What's a Millennium?

The word *millennium* means a period of 1,000 years. It can be any period of 1,000 years. For example, a millennium passed between the year A.D. 500 and the year A.D. 1500.

But most people use the word *millennium* to mean something else. They use it to refer to the years 1 to 1000, 1001 to 2000, 2001 to 3000 (we're not there yet!), and so on. The years 1 to 1000 are called the "first millennium," the years 1001 to 2000 the "second millennium," the years 2001 to 3000 will be the "third millennium," and so on. Can you see how this works?

The Millennium Is About to Change

You have probably already figured out that we are close to the end of the second millennium. Most people consider the year 1999 to be the last year of the second millennium. They consider the year 2000 to be the first year of the third millennium. At the stroke of midnight, December 31, 1999, they will celebrate the change, or turn, of the millennium.

There's only been one millennium change since the time humans first kept track of years. Can you think when that was?

Once in a Thousand Years

A change in the millennium is a rare event—it literally happens only "once in a thousand years." It makes things that happen "once in a lifetime" or "once in a blue moon" seem as if they happen all the time!

You're lucky to be alive when the millennium turns. For one thing, it will be the biggest celebration the world has ever known. Plans have been under way for years to make December 31, 1999, the night of the biggest New Year's party ever!

More important, the millennium is a time for reflection about ourselves, our country, and our world. We can look back at the past 1,000 years to see how things have changed. And we can look forward to the next 1,000 years and plan for what they will bring.

In everyone's life, there are a few once-in-a-lifetime events that stand out, that stay with them as long as they live. These events remain frozen in memory, as crystal clear as if they happened just a few moments ago. Even in old age, people remember exactly where they were, who they were with, and what they were doing when these once-in-a-lifetime events occurred. Midnight, December 31, 1999, will be such a moment for millions—perhaps billions—of people.

It will be such a moment for you, too. The change of the millennium will be one of your once-in-a-lifetime events. It may seem like a long time from now, but someday soon people will be asking you, "Where were you when the millennium changed?"

(continued)

Once in a Thousand Years *(continued)*

To help you think about the essay you just read, respond to the following questions.

1. (a) What is a millennium?

   (b) What do *most* people mean when they use the word *millennium*?

2. (a) Which millennium do we live in right now? (first? second? third?)

   (b) When did it start?

   (c) When do most people say it will end?

3. (a) What will the next millennium be called? (first? second? third?)

   (b) When do most people say it will start?

4. How often does the millennium change?

5. The writer of this essay says that people will always remember where they were when the millennium changed. Do you think this is true? Explain your answer.

A Millennium Brainstorm

How old will you be in the year 2000?

If you can answer this question, it means that you already know something about the upcoming turn of the millennium. Chances are, you know much more than that. Perhaps you've heard someone talk about it on a television show. Or someone you know has predicted what the world will be like in the year 2000. Maybe you've even thought about it yourself.

Focus | Think about what you already know about the turn of the millennium. Do you know when it will be? Do you know why people are talking about it? Record your knowledge in the following chart. List at least five things you already know about the turn of the millennium.

What I Know About the Turn of the Millennium
•
•
•
•
•

Asking and Answering Questions About the Turn of the Millennium

Has anyone ever said this to you?
"You'll never know if you don't ask!"
It's true. Asking questions is at the heart of learning. That's why your teachers are always asking you if you have any questions. When you get your answer, you learn something new.

To learn about the turn of the millennium, you'll need to ask questions. Chances are, the answers will surprise you. Why? Because the upcoming turn of the millennium is a unique event, and no one has ever experienced it before.

Focus | The following chart will help you formulate questions about the turn of the millennium. What's more, you'll get to think about how you can find out the answers to your questions. To complete the chart, list as many questions as you can in the left column. For each question, write down in the right column how you think you could find the answer. (It may be by reading a book, asking your teacher, or simply waiting until the millennium turns!)

When you've finished your chart, keep it. As each of your questions is answered, check it off.

Questions I Have About the Turn of the Millennium	How I Might Find the Answers to My Questions
•	•
•	•
•	•
•	•
•	•
•	•
•	•

LESSON 2: Millennium Words

Student Activity Sheet Disciplines and Levels

Student Activity Sheet	Discipline(s)	Level(s)
2A	language arts	B, C
2B	language arts	C
2C	language arts; mathematics	B, C

Lesson Snapshot

Working in pairs, students use reference tools to define "millennium words"—terms associated with the turn of the millennium (day, year, decade, etc.). They then explore these words further by identifying their origins. The individual terms are then related to one another through a table of time equivalents.

Objectives

- Students will explain that a single concept (the millennium) has a group of words associated with it.
- Students will add time- and millennium-related words to their vocabulary.
- Students will practice using reference tools to explore a group of related terms.
- Students will use a table and apply mathematics skills.
- Students will apply the following critical thinking skills: interpretation, application, analysis, synthesis, and evaluation.

Class Time Required

- 2 class periods

Materials Needed

- Student Activity Sheets 2A, 2B, and 2C
- dictionaries
- calculators (optional)

Lesson Plan

1. PREPARE

Before class you should . . .

- review the lesson materials;
- consider which students you would like to work together as partners;
- decide whether students will be allowed to use calculators to complete the calculations on Student Activity Sheet 3C.

2. TEACH

Focus

- Focus students' attention by writing the word *computer* on the chalkboard and challenging volunteers to identify computer words—specific terms that people need to know to understand computers (*memory, monitor, printer*, and so on).
- Depending on your class, you may wish to choose a different term to serve as the basis for this exercise. (You may also choose to repeat the exercise with one or more additional terms.)
- Point out to students that many subjects, concepts, and topics of study have a certain group of words associated with them, and that the millennium is no different. Tell them that they will engage in exercises to review some familiar words and learn some new ones that they can think of as millennium words.

Guide

- Organize the class into partners.

- Distribute one copy of Student Activity Sheet 2A and Student Activity Sheet 2B to each student. Provide each student with a dictionary.

- Assign student pairs the task of completing both activity sheets. Each pair should decide on their own how best to complete the task: working cooperatively on each activity sheet, or each working independently on a different activity sheet. (If students choose to work independently, tell them to check each other's work.)

- Before students begin, model for them how to find and read an etymology in the dictionary they will be using.

- As students work, explain to them how understanding a word's origin can help them better understand the word and remember its meaning.

- Be sure to circulate and monitor partners' working techniques.

Close

- Once students have completed their activity sheets, lead a class discussion about the activity. Randomly ask students to identify, define, and explain the origins of several of the millennium words.

- Write "Knew" and "New" as headings on the board. Lead the class to a consensus about which terms were familiar and which were new to them. Use these lists as springboards to further discussion.

- Explain to students that virtually all of the words they just studied are essentially mathematical terms, with values. Conclude by distributing Student Activity Sheet 2C as a homework assignment.

3. EVALUATE

- **Formal Evaluation** Collect and examine individual students' work on Student Activity Sheets 2A, 2B, and 2C.

- **Informal Evaluation** Observe individual students' attitudes and contributions during the partner work session.

- **Self-Evaluation** Have students consider these questions: How difficult is it for me to learn new words? and What could I do to make learning new terms easier for me?

4. EXTENSION AND ENRICHMENT

- Challenge students to a game of Word Wizard. Assign each millennium word a point value, and award students points for each time they can identify a time they read, hear, or use a millennium word outside of class.

- Further challenge students who enjoyed the mathematics work on Student Activity Sheet 2C with these questions: How many seconds are in a millennium? and How many days, hours, and seconds are left in the second millennium?

- Introduce the term *etymology* to students and explain its meaning and significance.

Teacher to Teacher   The definition and word origin activity sheets also work well as individual homework assignments.

Journal Activities

You may wish to assign the self-evaluation questions as journal topics. As an alternative, challenge students to further explore this question: What other words use the prefix *milli-*?

What Does It Mean?

How many words do you know? There are a mind-boggling 600,000 words in the English language. If you learned 24 new words a day—one every hour, night and day, without stopping—it would take you almost 70 years to learn them all!

Luckily, no one expects you to do that! But you will learn thousands and thousands of words in your lifetime. How do you manage to remember them all? One way is that you naturally tend to group words together. For example, see if you can figure out what all of these words have in common: *wheels, tires, chain, seat, brake, handlebars.* That's right, they're all "bicycle words."

Just as there is a group of words you need to know to think about bicycles, there is a group of words you need to know to think about the turn of the millennium. We can call them "millennium words."

Focus | Twelve millennium words are listed in the following chart. Some you are familiar with, and some may be new to you. Use a good dictionary and look up each one. Copy the definition of each word into the chart. Be careful—some of these words have more than one definition. Try to copy the one definition that is *most closely related* to the turn of millennium.

MILLENNIUM WORDS	
Word	**Definition**
1. calendar	
2. century	
3. day	
4. decade	
5. fin de siècle	
6. hour	
7. millennia	
8. millennial	
9. millennium	
10. minute	
11. second	
12. year	

Why Is It Called That?

A millennium is a period of 1,000 years. But why is it called that? Why isn't a period of 1,000 years called a "thousandyear" or a "lototime," or even a "thingamajig"?

For that matter, why is a day called a day, or a year called a year? Someone didn't just sit down and make our words up. There is a reason that each of our words is what it is. This reason lies in the origin, or source, of the word. Each individual word has its own origin. Word origins are usually listed in dictionaries, along with definitions.

Like every other word, "millennium words"—the words you need to know to understand the turn of the millennium—have their own origins. Knowing the origins of millennium words will help you understand the turn of the millennium itself.

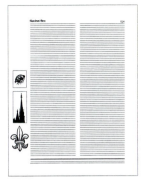

| Focus | Twelve millennium words are listed in the following chart. Use a dictionary to find each one's origin. Copy the origin into the chart. One has been done for you. |

MILLENNIUM WORDS	
Word	**Origin**
1. calendar	from the Latin word *calendarium,* meaning "account book"
2. century	
3. day	
4. decade	
5. fin de siècle	
6. hour	
7. millennia	
8. millennial	
9. millennium	
10. minute	
11. second	
12. year	

11 *Millennium: An Interdisciplinary Investigation*

How Are These Words Related?

Has anyone ever said anything like the following to you?

- "Just a second!"

- "Can you wait a minute?"

- "The movie is about two hours long."

- "We will have a test in two days."

- "Just two weeks until Christmas!"

Chances are you've heard these things, or something similar, many times before. We talk about time in many ways, and so often, because it's such a big part of our lives. Think to yourself: When was the last time you thought or talked about *when* something happened? It was probably "just a minute ago"!

You know that the words we use to talk about time—*second, minute, hour,* and so on—are related to each other. For example, there are 60 seconds in 1 minute, and 60 minutes in 1 hour. These relationships are called *equivalents.* Two things are said to be equivalent if they are equal. For instance, 60 seconds is said to be "equivalent to 1 minute" because 60 seconds equals 1 minute.

Focus Remind yourself of the way the words we use to talk about time are related by completing the following time equivalents table. If you need help completing the table, consult an almanac. Then complete the activities that follow.

Time Equivalents	
<u>60</u> seconds =	1 minute
<u>60</u> minutes =	1 hour
_____ hours =	1 day
_____ days =	1 year
_____ years =	1 decade
_____ decades =	1 century
_____ centuries =	1 millennium

(continued)

How Are These Words Related? *(continued)*

> Now use the table on the previous page to answer the following questions. The space beneath each question is there to give you room to do the math you'll need to come up with your answer. If your teacher says it's okay, go ahead and use a calculator.

1. How many centuries are in one millennium?

2. How many decades are in one millennium?

3. How many years are in one millennium?

4. How many seconds old will you be at midnight tonight?

5. How many years, days, hours, and seconds old will you be at midnight on December 31, 1999?

LESSON 3: Why Is the Millennium Turning?

Student Activity Sheet Disciplines and Levels

Student Activity Sheet	Discipline(s)	Level(s)
3A	science	B, C
3B	science	B, C

Lesson Snapshot

Students interpret diagrams of the earth and the earth in relation to the sun to understand exactly what is meant by a *day* and a *year*.

Objectives

- Students will explore the relationships between basic time measurements and the physical movement of the earth through space.
- Students will add forms of the words *revolve* and *rotate* to their vocabulary and interpret them in the context of the earth's movement.
- Students will apply the following critical thinking skills: application, analysis, and synthesis.

Class Time Required

- 1 class period

Materials Needed

- Student Activity Sheets 3A and 3B
- pencils or pens
- a globe
- a flashlight

Lesson Plan

1. PREPARE

Before class you should . . .

- review the lesson materials;
- make sure you have a globe and flashlight available for a classroom demonstration.

Before class students should . . .

- complete Student Activity Sheets 3A and 3B as homework.

2. TEACH

Focus

- Tell students that there's no such thing as a sunrise or a sunset. Challenge them to explain what you mean.
- Guide them into understanding that the sun doesn't rise or set, but remains relatively motionless, and that the rising and setting of the sun is only an appearance created by the rotation of the earth.

Guide

- Complete this demonstration to explain how daytime and nighttime are created. Turn off the lights in the classroom. Have a volunteer slowly rotate a globe counterclockwise as you shine a flashlight on it. Point out how some areas of the globe move into the light, creating a "sunrise," as areas on the far side of the globe move into shadow, creating a "sunset." Remind students of the term *axis* and point out the axis on the globe.
- Ensure student understanding of the earth's rotation and its relation to the concept of *day* before proceeding.
- Remind students that as the earth rotates on its axis, it also revolves in its orbit around the sun. Ask students how long it takes for the earth to complete one revolution (one year).
- Reinforce students' understanding of the earth's rotation and revolution by assigning one student to each of the following roles: sun, earth. Have the two students stand in a way that shows the relative

location of these objects. Then have the "earth" student walk to represent the earth revolving around the sun. Challenge the student to spin (rotate) as he or she orbits. Challenge the class to specify how many times the student should spin for each complete revolution (365). The "sun" student can hold a flashlight. As the "earth" student makes each revolution, have the class call out how many months and years have passed (three months for each quarter revolution).

Close

- Encourage students to memorize the two essential facts of the lesson by writing them on the chalkboard or recording them in their notebooks:

  1. The earth rotates on its axis once every 24 hours. One complete rotation is one day.

  2. The earth revolves around the sun, once every 365 days. One complete revolution is one year.

- Close by asking students how many times the earth revolves around the sun in one year, one decade, one century, and one millennium.

3. EVALUATE

- **Formal Evaluation** Collect and examine individual students' work on Student Activity Sheets 3A and 3B.

- **Informal Evaluation** When you can, ask individuals to briefly describe how the earth is moving at that moment.

- **Self-Evaluation** Have students consider these questions: Did I know what made a day and what made a year? and Did I learn best from the writing, the diagrams, or the in-class discussion?

4. EXTENSION AND ENRICHMENT

- Invite advanced students to prepare a presentation on why we have seasons. Have them present this to the class.

- Tell students that rotation and revolution are only two of three basic movements of the earth. Challenge them to find out what the third one is.

Teacher to Teacher   I'm always surprised that extremely basic information about the movement of the earth is not fully grasped by students. Don't assume that students have in their minds a good picture of the earth's movement.

Journal Activities

You may wish to assign the self-evaluation questions as journal topics. As an alternative, challenge students to further explore this question: Why is it important that I understand the movements of my planet?

Name _____

Date _____

Why Is the Millennium Turning?
Student Activity Sheet 3A

What's a Day, Anyway?

The upcoming turn of the millennium will be a historic moment in time. But what exactly is time? And how do we measure it?

A good place to start is with a unit of time you are very familiar with: a day. You know when yesterday was, when today is (right now), and when tomorrow will be. When you understand *why* yesterday was yesterday and why tomorrow will be tomorrow, you'll understand a lot more about what a day is. And you'll be a big step closer to understanding the turn of the millennium.

Focus | The following essay explains what a day *really* is. Read it, and study the accompanying diagram. Then answer the questions about the essay.

What's a Day, Anyway?

To understand what a day is, think about a basketball. That's right—a basketball.

Have you ever seen someone spin a basketball on her finger? Then you've seen a perfect model of the earth.

The earth spins, or *rotates*, just like a basketball balanced on a fingertip. Of course, the earth isn't held up by a giant finger. It floats in space. And the earth doesn't rotate nearly as fast as the basketball. A basketball spinning on a fingertip will rotate thousands of times in the time it takes the earth to rotate just once. But your planet *is* rotating right now, and you're rotating with it.

The earth rotates on its *axis*. An axis is an imaginary line running through a sphere. The axis of the spinning basketball is the imaginary line going up from the finger through the middle of the ball. The earth's axis extends through the earth from the North Pole to the South Pole.

It's the rotation of the earth on its axis that causes day and night. Imagine a flashlight beam pointing at a spinning basketball. The light can fall on just one half of the basketball at a time. That's the "day" side of the basketball. The "night" side of the basketball is the opposite side, in the shadow. The same is true of the earth. The side of the earth that faces the sun is in day. The side that faces away from the sun is in night. As the earth rotates on its axis, your community faces the sun, then faces away from it. It's day, then it's night, then it's day again, over and over and over, as the earth spins.

When you think of a day, you probably think of the time that the sun is shining on your part of the earth. And when you think of a night, you probably think of the time when your community is facing away from the sun and it is dark. But night is really part of the whole day.

So what's a day, anyway? A day is *one complete rotation of the earth on its axis*. It takes the earth 24 hours to complete one rotation, so there are 24 hours in a day.

(continued)

Name _____

Date _____

Why Is the Millennium Turning?
Student Activity Sheet 3A

What's a Day, Anyway? *(continued)*

The Earth's Rotation

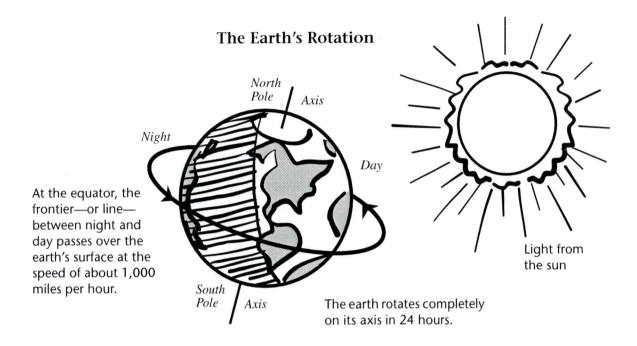

At the equator, the frontier—or line—between night and day passes over the earth's surface at the speed of about 1,000 miles per hour.

The earth rotates completely on its axis in 24 hours.

Light from the sun

1. What is the earth's axis?

2. How long does it take the earth to make one complete rotation on its axis?

3. About how fast does the earth spin at the equator?

4. In which direction does the earth spin?

5. What is a day?

6. A millennium is a period of 1,000 years. How many times does the earth rotate in one millennium?

Millennium: An Interdisciplinary Investigation

Name _____

Date _____

What's a Year, Dear?

At this very moment, you're flying through space. Your planet, Earth, is not just peacefully floating in one place. It's hurtling itself—and you, as a passenger—through the darkness at well over 60,000 miles per hour.

Where is it going? It's "running laps" around the sun. The earth *orbits,* or revolves around, the sun. It is this movement that we use to measure a year. So what's a year, dear? The answer is simple: *A year is the amount of time it takes the earth to complete one orbit, or revolution, around the sun.*

Focus | The diagram on the following page illustrates the orbit of the earth around the sun. Use the diagram to answer the questions that follow.

1. What is the earth's orbit?

2. How long does it take the earth to make one complete orbit of the sun?

3. How fast does the earth travel in its orbit?

4. On average, how far is the earth from the sun?

5. What is a year?

6. A millennium is a period of 1,000 years. How many times does the earth orbit the sun during one millennium?

7. How many more times will the earth orbit the sun between now and the year 2000?

(continued)

What's a Year, Dear? *(continued)*

The Earth's Revolution

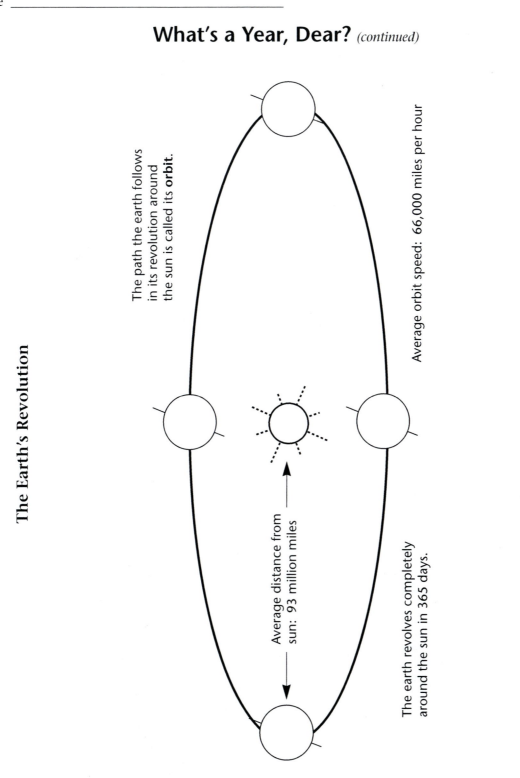

The path the earth follows in its revolution around the sun is called its **orbit**.

Average orbit speed: 66,000 miles per hour

Average distance from sun: 93 million miles

The earth revolves completely around the sun in 365 days.

LESSON 4: The Millennium and the Calendar

Student Activity Sheet Disciplines and Levels

Student Activity Sheet	Discipline(s)	Level(s)
4A	social studies	B, C
4B	social studies	A, B, C
4C	social studies; mathematics	B, C

Lesson Snapshot

Students learn what a calendar is and that we rely on the Gregorian calendar. The fact that the turn of the millennium is an event based on the Gregorian calendar is explained and emphasized. Students study the meanings of the abbreviations B.C., B.C.E., and A.D. in the context of the Gregorian calendar. Finally, they learn why we have leap years, and they consider whether the year 2000 will be a leap year.

Objectives

- Students will explain that the calendar they are familiar with is a particular calendar known as the Gregorian calendar.
- Students will investigate the meaning of the turn of the millennium in the context of the Gregorian calendar.
- Students will define B.C., B.C.E., and A.D.
- Students will describe the purpose of leap years.
- Students will determine whether the year 2000 will be a leap year.
- Students will apply the following critical thinking skills: interpretation, application, analysis, and synthesis.

Class Time Required

- 1 class period

Materials Needed

- Student Activity Sheets 4A, 4B, and 4C
- pencils or pens

Lesson Plan

1. PREPARE

Before class you should . . .

- review the lesson materials;
- consider which students you would like to work together in small groups or as partners.

Before class students should . . .

- complete Student Activity Sheet 4A and Student Activity Sheet 4B as preparatory homework.

2. TEACH

Focus

- Ask student volunteers to explain each of the following terms: B.C., B.C.E., A.D.
- Guide students into understanding that these abbreviations only have significance in the context of the Gregorian calendar.

Guide

- Lead a discussion about the Gregorian calendar. Based on their homework, students should be able to contribute to the discussion. Ask: What is the Gregorian calendar? Who developed it? When was it developed? Where is it used? Why is it the calendar we use today? How is it related to the turn of the millennium?
- Throughout, emphasize this basic fact: The turn of the millennium is an *event in the Gregorian calendar.*
- Emphasize, too, that the Gregorian calendar is only one of many possible calendars. Make

sure students understand that it is the one most widely used because of (1) the Christian heritage of Western Europe, and (2) the dominant role European culture has taken in many places in the world as a result of European expansion.

Close

- When you have finished the discussion about the Gregorian calendar, point out that the calendar is not perfect. Tell students that you'll give them a hint about the imperfection, and then take a slight leap.

- Once students have identified "leap year" as the imperfection, distribute one copy of Student Activity Sheet 4C to each student. Direct them to complete it individually as follow-up homework.

3. EVALUATE

- **Formal Evaluation** Collect and examine individual students' work on Student Activity Sheets 4A, 4B, and 4C.

- **Informal Evaluation** Observe individual students' attitudes and contributions during class discussions.

- **Self-Evaluation** Have students consider these questions: Why is the calendar important to me? and Why is it important that I am as familiar as possible with the Gregorian calendar?

4. EXTENSION AND ENRICHMENT

- As a group activity, have students make a "backwards" calendar that counts down to the turn of the millennium.

- Have interested students research and report on the ancient Babylonian, Mayan, and Aztec calendars.

Teacher to Teacher   The crux here is that our calendar is a cultural manifestation. Students need to learn that it represents one way of viewing and marking time, but that it isn't the only one or the best. They need to understand that the turn of the millennium is ultimately a Gregorian calendar event—no more, and no less.

Journal Activities

You may wish to assign the self-evaluation questions as journal topics. As an alternative, challenge students to further explore this question: What would life be like if there were no calendars?

The Gregorian Calendar

If you're like many people, the calendar runs your life. You start school on Mondays. You look forward to Fridays, because the calendar tells you that the weekend is then just a day away. You count the weeks to your birthday, or the months to summer vacation. Maybe your favorite store is closed on Sundays, or you know you'll get to see someone important to you on certain weekends.

Whatever events are important to you, the calendar tells you when they'll happen.

The biggest calendar event in history is the turn of the millennium. It will be noted on everybody's calendar. But if it weren't for the calendar, the millennium wouldn't be turning at all.

Focus To understand why the calendar is necessary for the millennium to turn, read the following essay. It also explains just what a calendar is and where the one you use came from. Read it carefully. Then answer the questions about the essay.

The Gregorian Calendar

A calendar is simply a way to measure the passage of time. Early in human history, people noticed that time changes in a regular way. They noticed that the sun rises and sets, the moon changes in a predictable fashion, and that seasons occur in the same cycle. Over time, they devised systems—calendars—to record and predict when these changes would occur.

Many ancient peoples made calendars. Some were based on the movement of stars, others on the change in seasons. Eventually, a calendar based on the sun was created. Each of these calendars was different— for example, each one had a different number of months and days in the year. Although they were different, they all tried to achieve the same goals of recording and predicting changes in the sky and the seasons.

The calendar that you are familiar with—with its 12 months (11 with 30 or 31 days and one with 28 days)—is a relatively new invention. It was developed in the 1580's by Pope Gregory XIII. It's called the Gregorian calendar, after its inventor.

Today, the Gregorian calendar is the most widely used calendar in the world. Virtually every country uses it as a common way of measuring time and agreeing on dates. However, it is important to remember that it is not the *only* calendar in the world. Islamic countries, for example, use a different calendar.

If it weren't for the Gregorian calendar, the millennium would not be turning. Why? Because the Gregorian calendar numbers years from the year that people think Jesus Christ was born. Dates after that year are called A.D. Dates before that year are called B.C. The end of the second millennium is two millennia, or 2,000 years, after when Jesus Christ is thought to have been born. In other words, the end of the second millennium, as measured by the Gregorian calendar, will be at the end of A.D. 2000.

So the turn of the millennium really means the turn of the millennium *as measured by the Gregorian calendar.* On other calendars, the millennium isn't turning at all. But since most people in the world use the Gregorian calendar, most people are marking their Gregorian calendars now for the turn of the millennium.

(continued)

The Gregorian Calendar (continued)

1. What is a calendar?

2. Why did people first develop calendars?

3. What is the most widely used calendar in the world today?

4. Where did the Gregorian calendar get its name?

5. Explain how the turn of the millennium is directly related to the widespread use of the Gregorian calendar.

As Easy As A-D-B-C-B-C-E

Soon, it will be the year 2000, right?
Wrong.
There is only one year 2000, right?
Wrong again.
Actually, it will be the year A.D. 2000. (You pronounce each letter—A-D—when you say it.) And there has been a year 2000 before—the year

2000 B.C. (You pronounce each letter—B-C— when you say it.) Other people might even call it the year 2000 B.C.E. (Again, pronounce each letter.)
What's going on here? It's really simple. And the information that follows will explain it to you.

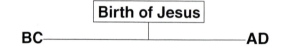

BC————————————AD

Focus | The box below explains the use of the A.D., B.C., and B.C.E. when talking about years. Study the information in the box. Then complete the activities that follow.

As Easy as A-D-B-C-B-C-E

The calendar we use today is based on the year that Christians believe Jesus Christ was born. Since there has to be a way to identify years both before and after this event, certain abbreviations are used.

B.C.: before Christ

- To indicate a year that occurred before the birth of Christ, the abbreviation B.C. is used. B.C. stands for "before Christ." For example, the year 1995 B.C. occurred 1,995 years before the year Jesus Christ is said to have been born. As you can see, the abbreviation B.C. is usually written **after** the year.

B.C.E.: before Christian era

- Instead of B.C., non-Christians sometimes prefer the abbreviation B.C.E. B.C.E. stands for "before the Christian era." 1995 B.C. and

1995 B.C.E. refer to the same year.

A.D.: anno Domini

- To indicate a year that occurred after the birth of Christ, the abbreviation A.D. is used. A.D. stands for *anno Domini*, a Latin phrase that means "in the year of our Lord." For example, the year A.D. 1995 occurred 1,995 years after the year Jesus Christ is said to have been born. As you can see, the abbreviation A.D. is usually written **before** the year.

- People often leave off the abbreviation A.D. If there is no abbreviation before or after a date, you can assume it means A.D. For example, if someone asks you when you were born, you might say "1987." You don't need to say "A.D. 1987"—it's obvious that you weren't born in 1987 B.C.!

(continued)

As Easy As A-D-B-C-B-C-E (continued)

1. On what event is our calendar based?

2. What does **B.C.** stand for?

3. What does **A.D.** stand for?

4. How are the abbreviations **B.C.** and **B.C.E.** similar?

5. Why are such abbreviations needed?

6. In the year **A.D.** 2000, when the second millennium ends, how many years will have passed since Jesus Christ is believed to have been born?

7. How is the turn of the millennium like a birthday?

Will We Leap into the New Millennium?

Were you born in a leap year? There's a 1 in 4 chance that you were. That's because a leap year is a special year that occurs once every four years.

They're not called leap years because everyone jumps all year! They're called leap years because there is a leap, or jump, in the calendar.

Will the year 2000 be a leap year? That's a good question, and the answer may surprise you. But first, you need to understand why we have leap years to begin with. That might surprise you, too.

FEBRUARY						
SUNDAY	MONDAY	TUESDAY	WEDNESDAY	THURSDAY	FRIDAY	SATURDAY
		1	2	3	4	5
6	7	8	9	10	11	12
13	14	15	16	17	18	19
20	21	22	23	24	25	26
27	28	(29)				

Focus The first box explains what leap years are and why we have them. Read it, then challenge yourself with the question that follows. Next, read the second box, which investigates whether the year 2000 will be a leap year.

A Leap Year

Our calendar is based on the year. We define a year as the time it takes for the earth to complete one orbit, or revolution, around the sun.

It might surprise you to learn that there are *not* 365 days in a year. There are actually 365 days, 5 hours, 48 minutes, and 48 seconds in a year. That's exactly how long it takes the earth to go around the sun. That's just about 365 and $\frac{1}{4}$ days.

Since it isn't practical to add $\frac{1}{4}$ day to the calendar each year, we do it all at once, by adding one day to the calendar every four years (four $\frac{1}{4}$ days equal one whole day). The year to which we

add the extra day is called a leap year. The day that is added each leap year is February 29.

But, if we did this every four years, the calendar would still be off. Why? because a year isn't *exactly* 365 $\frac{1}{4}$ days. It's about 11 minutes and 12 seconds short of that. So astronomers have determined that, to keep our calendar on track with the orbit of the earth around the sun, we don't need to add a leap year in century years (1700, 1800, 1900, and so on) *unless* that year is evenly divisible by 400.

Based on what you have just read, do you think the year 2000 will be a leap year? Explain your answer.

(continued)

Will We Leap into the New Millennium? *(continued)*

Will the Year 2000 Be a Leap Year?

It's a simple question.

Here's how the National Institute of Standards and Technology, the government agency in charge of measuring time, answers the question:

"The year 2000 will be a leap year. Century years (like 1900 and 2000) are only considered leap years if they are evenly divisible by 400. Therefore, 1700, 1800, and 1900 were not leap years, but the year 2000 will be a leap year.

To understand this, you need to know why leap years are necessary in the first place. Leap years are necessary because the actual length of a year is 365.242 days, not 365 days as commonly stated. Therefore, on years that are evenly divisible by 4 (like 1992, for example) an extra day is added to the calendar on February 29. However, since the year is slightly less than 365.25 (or 365 $\frac{1}{4}$) days long, adding an extra day every 4 years results in about 3 extra days being added over a period of 400 years. For this reason, only one out of every four century years is considered a leap year."

FEBRUARY						
SUNDAY	MONDAY	TUESDAY	WEDNESDAY	THURSDAY	FRIDAY	SATURDAY
		1	2	3	4	5
6	7	8	9	10	11	12
13	14	15	16	17	18	19
20	21	22	23	24	25	26
27	28	29				

Will the year 2000 be a leap year?

Explain your answer.

LESSON 5: The Turn of the Millennium Is Big News

Student Activity Sheet Disciplines and Levels

Student Activity Sheet	Discipline(s)	Level(s)
5A	social studies; language arts	B, C
5B	social studies	A, B, C

Lesson Snapshot

Students assess the newsworthiness of the turn of the millennium, using traditional journalistic criteria, and create clippings files of actual news stories about the turn of the millennium.

Objectives

- Students will develop an understanding of the concept of newsworthiness and apply journalistic criteria for newsworthiness.
- Students will read and interpret current periodical articles.
- Students will create a clippings file.
- Students will apply the following critical thinking skills: application, analysis, synthesis, and evaluation.

Class Time Required

- 1 class period

Materials Needed

- Student Activity Sheets 5A and 5B
- pencils or pens
- newspapers and newsmagazines
- loose-leaf notebooks and dividers
- tape or glue

Lesson Plan

1. PREPARE

Before class you should . . .

- review the lesson materials;
- consider which st udents you would like to work together in small groups.

2. TEACH

Focus

- Write "Dog Bites Man" and "Man Bites Dog" on the chalkboard. Ask students which headline would most likely catch their eye in a newspaper and why.
- Segue into a discussion of newsworthiness. Ask students why they think certain stories are included in the news and others aren't. Introduce the term *newsworthy* by having students identify its two parts.
- Explain that students will apply the concept of newsworthiness to the turn of the millennium.

Guide

- Organize the class into small groups. Explain that each group will function as the editorial board of a community newspaper.
- Distribute one copy of Student Activity Sheet 5A to each student. Direct students to follow it as a group but to complete it individually.
- Explain that students will simulate a meeting of a newspaper editorial board. Today, their task is to determine whether the turn of the millennium is a newsworthy event.
- Direct students to follow the instructions on the activity sheet.

Close

- Have a representative from each group explain why their group determined that the event was or was not newsworthy.

- Focus students' attention on the seven criteria themselves. Lead a class discussion about which criteria students think are more important than others. Ask: Should any of these standards be removed from the list? and Should additional standards be added? Have students explain their answers.

- Once the discussion is finished, point out that most newspaper editors have determined the turn of the millennium to be a newsworthy event. The proof is in the wealth of articles that have been published about it.

- Conclude by distributing Student Activity Sheet 5B as a homework assignment. Specify a time period over which students should update and maintain their clippings files.

3. EVALUATE

- **Formal Evaluation** Collect and examine individual students' work on Student Activity Sheet 5A and periodically collect and review students' clippings files.

- **Informal Evaluation** Observe individual students' attitudes and contributions during the group work period. When reviewing the clippings files, pay special attention to the quality of students' comments about the articles.

- **Self-Evaluation** Have students consider this question: How does reading newspapers and newsmagazines help me do well at school?

4. EXTENSION AND ENRICHMENT

- You might wish to have students draft a news story about the turn of the millennium. Several stories could be published in a student newspaper, *The Turn of the Millennium Times*.

- Expand the clippings files to include information students obtain from radio and television news stories. Students should write down summaries of what they hear.

Teacher to Teacher   You can have students create a class clippings file instead of individual ones. Award extra-credit points for bringing in articles. The class file makes a wonderful resource that students can use in their research and that you can use for additional lesson ideas, from creating a bulletin board to assigning oral presentations.

Journal Activities

You may wish to assign the self-evaluation question as a journal topic. As an alternative, challenge students to explore further this question: Would I like to work as a newspaper editor or reporter?

Is It Newsworthy?

Have you ever wondered how newspaper editors decide what stories to run and what stories not to run? The answer lies in a single word: newsworthiness.

A story is newsworthy if it is "worthy" of being included in the "news." Deciding whether a story is newsworthy can be difficult. One famous newspaper editor put it this way: "When a dog bites a man, that is not news, because it happens so often. But if a man bites a dog, that is news."

So one way to determine whether a story is newsworthy is how often it happens. But there are several other things to consider as well. In this lesson, you will determine whether the turn of the millennium is a newsworthy event.

Focus | Imagine you are an editor at your community newspaper. The turn of the millennium is coming up, and you're trying to decide what—if any—stories you should run about it. To help you decide, you apply the seven standards of newsworthiness. Explain why you think the turn of the millennium does or does not meet each of the seven standards listed here. Then complete the activity that follows.

Seven Standards of Newsworthiness

1. **Audience** Who is the audience, or readership, of your newspaper? Would a story or stories about the turn of the millennium be interesting to them? Why or why not?

2. **Impact** The impact of an event is its effect. Will the turn of the millennium have a large impact on your audience? Explain.

3. **Proximity** Proximity is the distance from an event to your audience. Is the turn of the millennium an event that is far removed from your readership, or will it occur in close proximity to them? Explain.

4. **Timeliness** Newspapers focus on reporting *current* events. Is the turn of the millennium a timely event, or will it happen too far in the past or too far in the future to interest or affect your readers? Explain.

(continued)

Is It Newsworthy? *(continued)*

5. **Prominence** Is the turn of the millennium a prominent, or famous, event? Will any famous people or places be involved in it? Assess the prominence of the turn of the millennium.

6. **Unusualness** A man biting a dog is news because it doesn't happen very often. Is this true of the turn of the millennium, or is it a common occurrence?

7. **Conflict** Many news stories involve conflict: Wars, elections, even sporting events involve conflict of one kind or another. Is there any conflict associated with the turn of the millennium? If so, what is it?

Now, to help you decide if the turn of the millennium is a newsworthy event, review your answers and complete the following chart with checkmarks.

Is the turn of the millennium newsworthy in terms of	Yes	No
1. Audience?		
2. Impact?		
3. Proximity?		
4. Timeliness?		
5. Prominence?		
6. Unusualness?		
7. Conflict?		

As a newspaper editor, will you run a story or stories about the turn of the millennium? Explain your decision.

Creating a Clippings File

Currently, there are about 3,000 newspapers in the United States. There are also thousands of magazines. Hundreds of them are printing stories on all aspects of the turn of the millennium. Hundreds more will. Why? Because the turn of the millennium is Big News.

The stories are about more topics than you might imagine. They range from stories on a debate over when the new millennium will actually begin, to stories on how people plan to celebrate the big event. Magazines aimed at people in specific professions run stories about how the change in the millennium might affect their jobs. (One magazine for fishermen ran a story about how millennium New Year's parties on boats might affect fishing in coastal waters.) Some stories are about what life might be like in the third millennium. Whatever they're about, stories on the turn of the millennium can make fascinating reading.

Focus No one person can read everything that has been and will be written about the turn of the millennium, but you can make a good start. This lesson will guide you in making a clippings file of stories about the turn of the millennium.

Making a Clippings File About the Turn of the Millennium

To make your clippings file about the turn of the millennium, follow these steps.

1. **Get a Notebook** You'll need something to keep your clippings in. A loose-leaf notebook works best, since you can add new clippings easily and rearrange them when you need to.

2. **Title Your Notebook** Give your clippings file a title. It can be straightforward and professional, like "Articles About the Turn of the Millennium," or fun, like "Millions of Words About the Millennium."

3. **Keep an Eye Out** You should read newspapers and magazines regularly. Read your local newspaper at least once a week, and try to read it every day. Strive to read at least one or two newsmagazines every month.

4. **Clip Articles** When you come across an article that has to do with the turn of the millennium, clip it out. (First, make sure that you get permission.) If you can't clip an article—if you find it in the library, for instance—then copy it instead.

5. **Post the Articles in Your Notebook** Glue or tape each article on a separate piece of notebook paper and add it to your notebook. Make sure you have carefully read each article you add to your notebook.

6. **Explain Each Article** On the piece of paper on which each article is glued, write a few words to record your thoughts about your article. Was it particularly interesting for some reason? Did it relate to something you learned at school? By recording your thoughts, you will get the most out of each article and your entire clippings file.

7. **Organize Your Notebook** As your notebook grows, you will see how different articles are related in some way. Using dividers, organize your notebook in a logical way. For example, you  might have one section of articles about how people are planning to celebrate the turn of the millennium, another section with articles about how the change in the year will affect computers, and so on.

8. **Keep Your Notebook** Why? Because someday it will be a valuable historical document: a record of what people wrote—and what you thought—during one of the most spectacular events in human history.

LESSON 6: How Important Is the Turn of the Millennium?

Student Activity Sheet Disciplines and Levels

Student Activity Sheet	Discipline(s)	Level(s)
6A	social studies; language arts	A, B, C
6B	social studies	B, C

Lesson Snapshot

Students respond to other middle-school-age students' responses to the question, Why do you think people consider the year 2000 and the turn of the millennium to be so important? Then they respond to the question themselves. Students also learn that the turn of the millennium has no significance, and doesn't even exist, to millions of people around the world who don't live under the Gregorian calendar.

Objectives

- Students will evaluate other young people's assessments of the importance of the turn of the millennium.

- Students will assess the importance of the turn of the millennium themselves.

- Students will explain why the turn of the millennium does not exist for people who don't follow the Gregorian calendar.

- Students will apply the following critical thinking skills: analysis and evaluation.

Class Time Required

- 1 class period

Materials Needed

- Student Activity Sheets 6A and 6B
- pencils or pens

Lesson Plan

1. PREPARE

Before class you should . . .

- review the lesson materials;

- consider whether you would like students to complete the student activity sheets individually or as partners.

Before class students should . . .

- complete Student Activity Sheet 6A as preparatory homework.

2. TEACH

Focus

- Launch the lesson by writing "What's all the fuss about the turn of the millennium?" or a similar, informal, question on the chalkboard.

- Invite student responses to the question. Record a few salient ones under the question on the board.

Guide

- Call students' attention to their completed Student Activity Sheet 6A.

- Call on a volunteer to read each quotation aloud in turn. After each one is read, guide the class into (1) understanding what the student who made the statement meant; (2) finding out whether and why students agree or disagree with the statement, and; (3) using the statement as a springboard to further discussion.

- Finally, have student volunteers share their responses to the last question on the student activity sheet. Write down several on the board. Once they are listed, guide students in categorizing the responses. Create a final, master list of "Reasons People Find the Millennium Important" that incorporates the reasons identified by your students and the students quoted on the activity sheet.

- Create a second heading on the board: "Reasons People Find the Millennium Unimportant." Write "It doesn't exist for them" as the first item on the list, and challenge the class to explain the significance.

- Review the essential lesson of Student Activity Sheet 6B with students: that the turn of the millennium is an event on the Gregorian calendar, and many people in the world don't follow this calendar.

Close

- Conclude by emphasizing how the millennium has great meaning for some people, little meaning to others, and no meaning to still others.

- Collect student activity sheets for evaluation.

3. EVALUATE

- **Formal Evaluation** Collect and examine individual students' work on Student Activity Sheets 6A and 6B.

- **Informal Evaluation** Observe individual students' attitudes and contributions during the group discussion period.

- **Self-Evaluation** Have students consider these questions: How important is learning about the turn of the millennium to me? and What could I have done to contribute more to the class discussion?

4. EXTENSION AND ENRICHMENT

- Invite interested students to learn more about non-Gregorian calendars and share them with the class.

- Challenge a small team of students to color a world map to show where the Gregorian calendar is and isn't used.

Teacher to Teacher The kids like responding to the quotes of their peers. I would assign this lesson to partners, so the two real students and the ones quoted on the activity sheet can get a dialogue or a conversation going. It sounds odd, but it works because the two real kids can sort of "talk about" the kid who is quoted on the activity sheet!

Journal Activities

You may wish to assign the self-evaluation questions as journal topics. As an alternative, challenge students to further explore this question: Would it be better if everyone in the world followed the same calendar?

Name _____

Date _____

How Important Is the Turn of the Millennium?
Student Activity Sheet 6A

"That's When the Future Begins"

Try this experiment: Ask your parents if, when they were children, they ever figured out how old they would be in the year 2000. There's a good chance that they'll say yes. Perhaps you've figured out how old you will be, too.

Why do you think this is so? The answer is that the year 2000 and the turn of the millen-nium holds a special significance to most people. For many years—since when your grandparents were children, and even earlier—the year 2000 and the turn of the millennium has seemed like an important turning point. The question is, Why?

Focus | The following box contains answers by middle-school students to a question about why the year 2000 and the turn of the millennium seem so important. As you read the answers, think about which ones you agree with. Then answer the questions that follow.

Question:

Why do you think people consider the year 2000 and the turn of the millen-nium to be so important?

Answers by middle-school students:

"It's going to be 2000-and-something for a long time, just like the year was 1000-and-some-thing for a long time. So it's important when it starts." —Benito

"Because 1,000 years is such a big time." —Missy

"It's like a big birthday, and birthdays are important." —Elizabeth

"I think it's important because there will be a new day, a new decade, a new century, and a new millennium all at once." —Robby

"Everything on TV talks about 'How in the year 2000 life will be like this' or 'By the year 2000' and stuff. It's like that's when the future begins." —Vernon

"People are making a big deal out of it because people always make a big deal out of time, like with watches and calendars and schedules." —Nadia

"It's like trying to watch a clock move. Some-times I watch this big clock in our living room to see if I can see the minute hand move. If you look at it a long time, you really can. Sometimes I watch this other clock that's a digital clock to see if I can be looking at it when the minute changes or the hour. When it's 2000 it'll be really neat to watch the clock turn and then it's a new millennium." —Charlie

"2000 is a special number, like 1000 or 100. . . . You know, it's not just a regular number like 6 or 7." —Lionel

---

(continued)

Name _____ How Important Is the Turn of the Millennium?

Date _____ **Student Activity Sheet 6A**

"That's When the Future Begins" *(continued)*

1. As you read through the answers, which one struck you as the most interesting? Why?

2. Reread the question and Elizabeth's answer to it (it's the third answer). Explain what you think she means by the turn of the millennium being "like a big birthday."

3. How are Robby's and Benito's answers to the question similar?

4. What do you think Lionel means when he says that "2000 is a special number"?

5. Number the answers in the box from 1 to 8 to show what you think is the best answer, the second-best answer, and so on.

6. Do any of the answers strike you as not being true or accurate about the year 2000 and the turn of the millennium? Explain.

7. Now it's your turn: Why do *you* think people consider the year 2000 and the turn of the millennium to be so important?

Name _____

Date _____

How Important Is the Turn of the Millennium?
Student Activity Sheet 6B

"To Us It's Just Another Day"

The year 2000 and the turn of the millennium is a worldwide event of historic importance that everyone on the planet will celebrate. Right?

Wrong.

Although millions of people think of the turn of the millennium as a watershed, or important historical turning point, millions of others will think of it as "just another day." Why do they feel this way? The answer is that not everyone in the world measures time using the calendar that we do. Because the turn of the millennium is based on our calendar, those people who don't use our calendar don't think of the year 2000 as the turn of the millennium—or even the year 2000 at all.

Focus | In the following box, three examples of why the turn of the millennium is "just another day" to others are explained. Read them. Then complete the activities that follow.

Just Another Day

For people who measure time differently from the way we do, the turn of the millennium doesn't stand out on the calendar. In fact, it isn't on their calendar at all. Consider the following:

The Chinese Calendar

The oldest calendar that is still in use is the Chinese calendar. The first year in the calendar is what we would call 2637 B.C., which is the year a legendary Chinese emperor is believed to have created the calendar.

The Chinese calendar organizes time into cycles of 60 years. A year is said to be "a certain year in a certain cycle." 2637 B.C. was "the first year in the first cycle." The year 2577 (60 years later) was "the first year in the second cycle," and so on. In addition, each year is assigned an animal name based on the Chinese zodiac. Twelve animals appear in this order: rat, ox, tiger, hare, dragon, snake, horse, sheep, monkey, rooster, dog, and pig. What will the year 2000 be? The Year of the Dragon.

The Hebrew Calendar

The Hebrew calendar is supposed to begin with the creation of the universe, a date equivalent to our year of 3660 B.C. So, for those people following the Hebrew calendar, our year 2000 will occur during their year 5760—which is clearly not a turn of a millennium.

The Islamic Calendar

The Islamic calendar measures time from the prophet Muhammad's flight from the city of Mecca to the city of Medina. In the Muslim faith, this flight is called the *Hegira* (pilgrimage). In our calendar, it took place in A.D. 622. In the Islamic calendar, time is divided into 30-year cycles, and the year is only 354 days long. The year 2000 in our calendar will be the year 1420 in the Muslim calendar.

Native American Views of Time

Many Native American groups follow traditional ways of viewing time, which can be very different from our calendar system. Oren Lyons, a leader of the Turtle Clan of the Onondaga Nation, put it this way: "We appreciate that the turning of the year 2000 represents some sort of [important date] from the perspective of our white brothers, but to us it's just another day."

(continued)

"To Us It's Just Another Day" *(continued)*

1. What cycle and what year will the year 2000 be in the Chinese calendar?

2. From what event does the Islamic calendar begin?

3. What event marks the beginning of the Hebrew calendar?

4. Why do you think the turning of the year 2000 is "just another day" to the people of the Onondaga nation?

5. There are about 6 billion people on earth. Conduct research to find out about how many people live under calendars that do not accept the year 2000 as the turn of the millennium.

6. Despite the differences among the world's calendars, most nations use the same calendar we do as their official calendar. Why do you think this is so?

LESSON 7: Organizing Your Thoughts About the Turn of the Millennium

Student Activity Sheet Disciplines and Levels

Student Activity Sheet	Discipline(s)	Level(s)
7A	interdisciplinary	A, B, C
7B	interdisciplinary	A, B, C

Lesson Snapshot

Students complete a graphic organizer about Unit 1 materials by answering specific questions. They are given a generic graphic organizer about the turn of the millennium in general to keep and add to throughout the course of their study.

Objectives

- Students will organize their thoughts and their learning about the turn of the millennium in a visual manner.
- Students will apply the following critical thinking skills: application and synthesis.

Class Time Required

- 1 class period

Materials Needed

- Student Activity Sheets 7A and 7B
- pencils or pens

Lesson Plan

1. PREPARE

Before class you should . . .
- review the lesson materials.

2. TEACH

Focus
- Ask students to list examples of how information is presented visually. Encourage them to list such things as maps, charts, graphs, and so on.

- Ask them why information is presented this way. Guide them into seeing that such visual presentations can convey a great deal of information in simple, easy-to-understand ways.

- Inform students that they will have the opportunity to organize the information that they learn about the turn of the millennium in a unique visual format.

Guide
- Organize the class into partners.

- Distribute one copy of Student Activity Sheet 7A to each student. Direct students to work together to complete the activities, but to make and keep their own individual copies. Allow students sufficient time to complete their tasks.

- As students work, circulate and remind individual pairs of when they learned the answer to each question and where they can look to remind themselves of the answer. If some of the questions have not been addressed, conduct mini-lessons during the work period to teach students the answers.

Close
- Collect students' completed activity sheets.

- Distribute one copy of Student Activity Sheet 7B to each student.

- Explain that the sheet you have just distributed is similar to the one they just completed.

- Have students read the directions to the activity sheet, and make sure they understand them.

- Ensure that students understand that they are responsible for keeping the activity sheet and updating it on a regular basis.

3. EVALUATE

- **Formal Evaluation** Collect and examine individual students' work on Student Activity Sheet 7A.

- **Informal Evaluation** Periodically review with students their additions to Student Activity Sheet 7B.

- **Self-Evaluation** Have students consider these questions: Have I been learning all I should about the turn of the millennium? and What can I do to help me remember more of what I learn in class?

4. EXTENSION AND ENRICHMENT

- Encourage students to create similar graphic organizers in your class and others to help them with their learning.

Teacher to Teacher   Graphic organizers are always useful. But you might need to help students appropriately classify questions for the second one. They sometimes want to list "why" questions as "what" questions. Also, you should encourage them to make links between the different categories.

Journal Activities

You may wish to assign the self-evaluation questions as journal topics. As an alternative, challenge students to explore further this question: Why is it important that I can organize information into different categories, like *who, what, when, where, why,* and *how*?

Name _____

Date _____

Organizing Your Thoughts Visually

Although it's just a single, simple moment in time, the turn of the millennium is a not just a single, simple event. To fully understand the turn of the millennium, you have to think about it in many different ways. A good way to help you do this—and to remember what you think—is to organize your thoughts visually.

Focus | The diagram here will help you organize what you have already learned about the turn of the millennium. To complete it, answer the question in each "bubble."

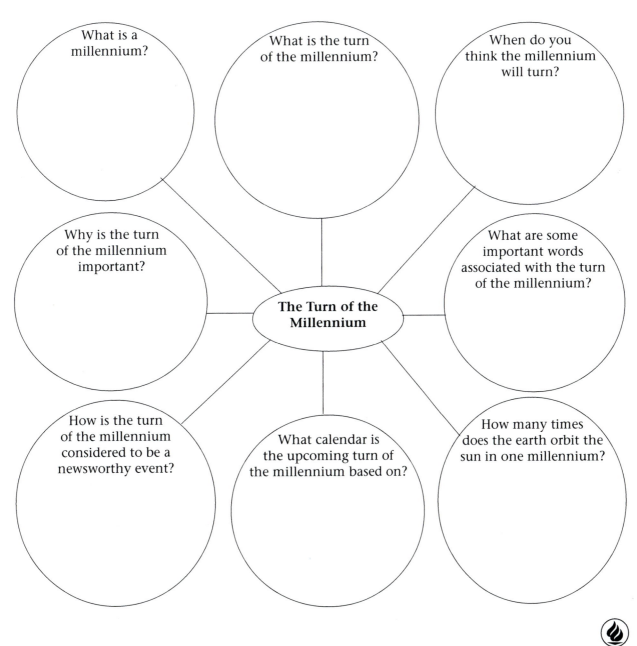

Who, What, Where, When, Why, and How?

As you learn more and more about the turn of the millennium, it is important to keep track of what you learn. The following diagram will help you.

Focus

> The diagram here is based on the basic questions Who? What? Where? When? Why? and How? As you learn about the turn of the millennium, record what you learn in the appropriate box. For example, if you discover *how* the turn of the millennium will be celebrated in your community, write it in the "How" box. When you learn *why* the turn of the millennium is important to many people, write it in the "Why" box. Try to record as much information as you can.

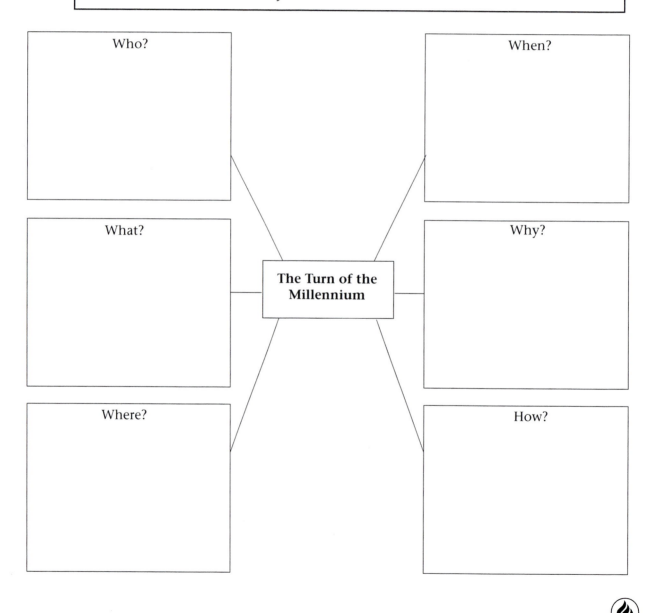

Who?

When?

What?

Why?

The Turn of the Millennium

Where?

How?

Unit II

THE MILLENNIUM THAT WAS

LESSON 8: Looking Back on the Second Millennium

Student Activity Sheet Disciplines and Levels

Student Activity Sheet	Discipline(s)	Level(s)
8A	social studies	A, B, C
8B	social studies	A, B, C
8C	social studies; mathematics	B, C
8D	social studies	A, B, C
8E	social studies	C

Lesson Snapshot

Students begin by engaging in a variety of activities to help them visualize just how long and full a historical period the second millennium was. Then students compare and contrast aspects of life 1,000 years ago with life today. Next, they focus on the dramatic population change of the last 1,000 years. Finally, they construct a time line of the salient events of the second millennium and analyze them from the perspective of a historian.

Objectives

- Students will visualize the great length of time of one millennium and appreciate how much can happen in 1,000 years.
- Students will compare and contrast aspects of life in A.D. 1000 and A.D. 2000.
- Students will analyze the change in the world's population over the course of the second millennium.
- Students will construct a time line of the second millennium.
- Students will analyze the second millennium from a historian's perspective.
- Students will apply the following critical thinking skills: interpretation, application, analysis, synthesis, and evaluation.

Class Time Required

- approximately 3 class periods

Materials Needed

- Student Activity Sheets 8A, 8B, 8C, 8D, and 8E
- calculators (optional)
- metersticks
- materials to construct a bulletin board time line (construction paper, scissors, markers, etc.)
- almanacs and encyclopedias
- a time line of the second millennium (available in almanacs and encyclopedias)

Lesson Plan

1. PREPARE

Before class you should . . .

- review the lesson materials;
- consider which students you would like to work together in partners and small groups;
- decide which projects to complete.

Before class students should . . .

- complete Student Activity Sheet 8A as preparatory homework.

2. TEACH

Focus

- Write "A.D. 1000 to A.D. 2000" on the chalkboard and ask students what happened during this time period.

- Guide students into identifying several major events, but then write "A lot!" on the board. Emphasize the sheer number and diversity of events that have happened over this large time span.

- Point out that so much has happened *because* it's such a long time period. Invite students to share their experiences as they complete the activities on Student Activity Sheet 8A.

Guide

- Point out to students that the world is very different now from the way it was 1,000 years ago, but that it is also the same in many ways.

- Organize the class into partners.

- Distribute one copy of Student Activity Sheet 8B to each student pair. Guide students in completing the sheet cooperatively. You may choose to conduct the final activity on the sheet as a class exercise, drawing a Venn diagram on the chalkboard.

- Assign Student Activity Sheet 8C as homework.

- Student Activity Sheet 8D guides students in a class project to construct a time line of the second millennium on the classroom bulletin board. Carefully assign student groupings to maximize group effectiveness. You will need to guide students in identifying which events to include. Promote multiculturalism by encouraging students to consider and include important non-European events.

- Student Activity Sheet 8E is for advanced students. If the class has constructed a time line, you can guide the students through the activity sheet as a whole, using the class time line as a source. Alternatively, consider assigning this difficult activity sheet as extra credit to student pairs.

Close

- Conclude the lesson by leading a class discussion based on this question: What can we learn by looking back on the second millennium?

- Emphasize the value of studying history as a way to learn about the present. Point out that studying history is really just a way to learn from past mistakes.

- Encourage students to take a larger view of history as something beyond a series of events and dates, and to seize upon the turn of the millennium as an opportunity to view life on earth in a larger context.

3. EVALUATE

- **Formal Evaluation** Collect and examine individual students' work on Student Activity Sheets 8A and 8C.

- **Informal Evaluation** Observe individual students' attitudes and contributions during the construction of the class time line and during class discussion periods.

- **Self-Evaluation** Have students consider these questions: How does what I have learned help me understand my own place in history? and Which activity did I enjoy the most, and why?

4. EXTENSION AND ENRICHMENT

- Use Student Activity Sheet 8E as an extension and enrichment activity.

- Have groups perform skits to dramatize the differences in the lives of young people 1,000 years ago and today.

Teacher to Teacher   Do the 1,000-Year Walk as a group—see how far you can get! The trick is to keep it verbal—talking to students, asking questions, cracking jokes.

The population worksheet is a good springboard to broader discussions of population, environmentalism, and current events, like famines.

The time-line project is a major undertaking. Make sure you emphasize that probably no two people would agree on what events are the most important, so students shouldn't feel pressured to identify the "right" events. It is important to give them a lot of guidance in their research, steering them to appropriate reference materials. Time lines in almanacs are a good bet.

Journal Activities

You may wish to assign the self-evaluation questions as journal topics. As an alternative, challenge students to explore further this question: What was a typical day like for a person my age 1,000 years ago?

Imagining 1,000 Years

A millennium is a long time. A very long time. It can be difficult, even mind-boggling, to imagine just how long 1,000 years is. But there are some fun ways to do it. A good place to start is with your own life. Have you ever been hungry, and had to wait another 20 minutes before dinner was ready? That 20 minutes seemed like a long wait at the time. Or have you ever impatiently awaited the arrival of a special day, like your birthday, or a holiday? Imagine having to wait 1,000 years for something!

Focus	The following exercises will help you appreciate just how long 1,000 years is. Do them in any order you wish. Then complete the final activity.

A 1,000-Year Walk

Pick a nice day, a safe area, and go for a walk. As you walk, count your steps. Your goal is to take 1,000 steps (you'll walk about half a mile). To help you keep count, you might want to take a pen and paper and make tally marks (卌) for every 100 steps.

You'll do more than count your steps. For each step you take, try to imagine one year. Think about all the things that can happen in one year. When you finish your walk, think about how much can happen in 1,000 years.

A 1,000-Year Ruler

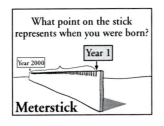

What point on the stick represents when you were born?

Year 2000

Year 1

Meterstick

Borrow a meter-stick from your teacher. The smallest measurements marked on the stick are milli-meters. There are 1,000 millimeters in a meter. (They're called *millimeters* because *milli-* means 1,000. The word millimeter shares this word part with *millennium*, which means one thousand years.)

Place the ruler sideways in front of you, and think of it as a time line. Each millimeter represents one year, so the whole meterstick represents 1,000 years. Ask yourself these questions: About how many millimeters are there in one person's lifetime? What markings on the meterstick indicate decades and centuries? If the end of the meter stick represents the year 2000, what point on the meterstick represents when you were born?

1,000 Years in 42 Days

Using a current calendar, find out what day it was 42 days ago. Try to remember what you were doing on that day. Family members, friends, and your teacher can help you remember.

Now imagine that time is somehow accelerated, so that each year rushes by in just an hour. If this happened, 1,000 years would go by in about 42 days. Think of how full your life has been, and how many things have happened, in just the past 42 days. That's about 1,000 hours in one life (yours). Imagine how much can happen in 1,000 *years,* in *billions* of lives!

1,000 Years in 1,000 Pages

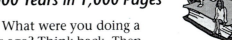

What were you doing a year ago? Think back. Then think about everything that's happened to you since then. It's been a lot: events with your family and friends; new teachers and class projects; happy times; tough times.

Now try to imagine writing everything that has happened to you over the past year on just one page. It would be impossible, of course (unless you used really, really small handwriting!). But you could just list the most important events.

Next, find a big, BIG book (an unabridged dictionary will work well). Turn to page 1,000 and hold 1,000 pages in your hand. Imagine that on each page is written all the events that happened to everybody in one year. Can you see how many billions of things can happen in 1,000 years?⸱⸱⸱⸱⸱⸱ *(continued)*

Imagining 1,000 Years (continued)

Thinking About 1,000 Years

1. Which of the exercises did you actually do? Write them and the date that you did them in the following chart.

Activity	Did I Do It? (Yes or No)	Date Done
A 1,000-Year Walk		
A 1,000-Year Ruler		
1,000 Years in 42 Days		
1,000 Years in 1,000 Pages		

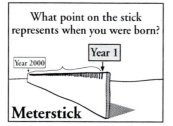

2. Which activity best helped you to imagine how long 1,000 years is? Explain your answer.

Then and Now

A lot can happen in a thousand years. And a lot *has* happened during the second millennium.

The truth is, the world has changed a lot since the year A.D. 1000. If you were to travel back to that year in a time machine, you could see firsthand just how different the world was. But you might be surprised to see how *little* has changed, too. People are people, after all, whether they lived in the year A.D. 1000 or live in the year A.D. 2000. Many of the things you would see as you emerged from your time machine would be familiar to you. What do you think would be the same, and what would be different?

Focus To help you compare the world of A.D. 1000 and the world of A.D. 2000, think about each item in the box that follows. Copy each item into the chart on the following page to show whether it tells about the world of 1,000 years ago, the world of today, or both worlds.

About 1.2 billion people live on earth.   About 6 billion people live on earth.

Books are printed by machine.   Books are written.

Europeans visit North America.   Forests cover most of Europe.

Most people do not live beyond the age of 30.

North America is populated only by Indians.   People fall in love.

People play basketball.   People play sports.   People travel by car.

People use animals to do work for them.   People use electricity.

People use machines to do work for them.   People use telephones.

Walking and animal-drawn carts are the most common forms of transportation.

Wood is the most important source of fuel.

(continued)

Then and Now *(continued)*

A Millennium Ago (A.D. 1000)	Today (A.D. 2000)	A Millennium Ago *and* Today

Now add at least three items of your own choosing to each column in the chart.

Interpreting a Population Line Graph

Without a doubt, one of the biggest changes to have occurred over the last millennium is the sheer number of people living on the face of the earth. A thousand years ago, no one could imagine how many people would be alive today. The numbers are staggering.

Focus | The following line graph shows the change in the world's population over the last millennium. Study the graph and use it to answer the questions that follow.

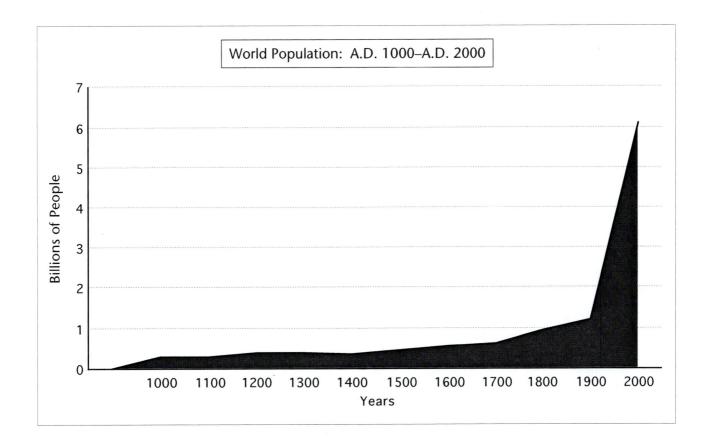

(continued)

Interpreting a Population Line Graph *(continued)*

1. What was the population of the world in A.D. 1000, at the beginning of the second millennium?

2. What was the population of the world in A.D. 1500, at the middle of the second millennium?

3. What is the world's population in A.D. 2000, at the end of the second millennium?

4. (a) By how much has the population changed in 1,000 years?

   (b) By what percentage has the population changed in 1,000 years?

5. (a) What general trend does the graph show?

   (b) If this trend were to continue, what would you estimate the world's population to be at the end of the third millennium (A.D. 3000)?

Creating a Time Line

One historian has pointed out a unique opportunity that the turn of the millennium provides us: "The approach of the year 2000 makes the present a [particularly] good time for taking stock of our last thousand years of history, asking where they have led us. . . ."

This is a perfect time for "taking stock" of the last millennium. What have the last 1,000 years meant for humanity? Where have they led us? Are we going in the right directions?

To answer these questions, we must first form a picture of what the last 1,000 years have brought. Of course, no one can know everything about the history of such a long span of time. But by identifying major events of the last 1,000 years, we can begin to form a picture of the second millennium, and start to answer the questions about the second millennium that the end of it has raised.

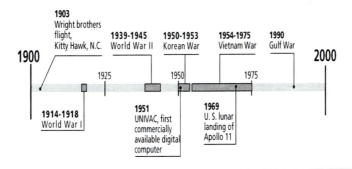

Focus | To help you form a picture of the last 1,000 years, create a time line by taking the following steps.

1. Work with your teacher to organize the class into 10 research groups.

2. Each group will be responsible for making a time line of the major events of one century of the second millennium (the 1000's, the 1100's, the 1200's, and so on). Once each group is finished, the time lines will be joined on the bulletin board to make one large bulletin-board time line of the entire second millennium.

3. Each group should accomplish these tasks:

   • Conduct research to identify the 10 *most important* events that occurred during their century. (A good way to determine which events are the most important is to consider their long-term effects. For example, the development of the printing press in the 1400's has had major long-term effects.) Each group should list their 10 events, along with the date that each occurred.

   • Identify the significance of each event. In other words, each group should write

   a sentence explaining why each event on their list is important.

4. Once each group has completed its list, a representative from each group should meet to agree on a design for the completed bulletin-board time line. Consider such things as how long the completed time line will be, how much space will be allocated to each year, how decades and centuries will be marked, and so on.

5. Each group should construct and illustrate their part of the time line so it matches the other groups'. Each time line should include the date of each event, the name of each event, and a description of why the event was important. At least two events from each section of the time line should be illustrated.

6. Group representatives should work together to construct the final time line on the bulletin board and give it an appropriate title.

Thinking About the Last 1,000 Years

What's the most important thing that has ever happened to you?

It's a tough question.

After all, in everybody's life, there are many, many events that are personaly very important. It is difficult, if not impossible, to single out the one most important event.

And that's a problem historians face. As they look back over the second millennium and try to make sense of it, they are overwhelmed by the sheer number of important things that have happened. Dozens, even hundreds or thousands, of these events have transformed the world. Just think about Columbus coming to America, inventions like the airplane and the computer, World War II . . . the list is endless. So how can historians make sense of the second millennium?

The answer is that they try to do two major things. One, they try to identify the events that have affected the most people for the longest amount of time. For example, a small battle in Europe in the 1300's was certainly important to the people in it at the time, but it does not really affect our world today. On the other hand, the invention of the automobile in the 1900's has changed the landscape of the world.

A second thing historians do is look for trends, or general directions, in the course of history. For example, two important trends are urbanization (more people living in urban areas, or cities) and the development of larger nations to replace kingdoms.

By identifying major events and trends, historians can begin to develop a picture of what life in the second millennium has meant for humankind.

Focus | The following questions are designed to guide you in finding the major events and trends of the past 1,000 years. As you work through them, imagine that you are a historian. Your goal is to write a group of phrases that accurately describe the second millennium. You will need to use a time line of the second millennium to complete your task.

1. Of all the events listed on the time line, which three seem to you to have affected the most people for the longest time? List them here, along with an explanation of how each has had a great effect.

   (a)

   (b)

   (c)

(continued)

Thinking About the Last 1,000 Years *(continued)*

2. If you had to choose the single most important event of the second millennium, what would you say it was? Explain the reason for your choice.

3. Can you detect any trends on the time line? If so, identify them.

4. One historian said the one phrase that best sums up the second millennium is "a time of great change." Do you agree with this statement? Why or why not?

5. What phrases would you use if you had to try to sum up the last 1,000 years? Try to list at least three.

LESSON 9: When a Millennium Turns

Student Activity Sheet Disciplines and Levels

Student Activity Sheet	Discipline(s)	Level(s)
9A	social studies	B, C

Lesson Snapshot

As preparatory homework, students read and respond individually to a brief article that compares and contrasts the last turn of the millennium with the current one. In class, they focus on the differences and volunteer ideas as to why they exist.

Objectives

- Students will understand that the millennium has turned just once before.
- Students will describe the differences between the world of A.D. 1000 and the world of today.
- Students will compare and contrast the turn of the first millennium and the turn of the second millennium.
- Students will apply the following critical thinking skills: interpretation and analysis.

Class Time Required

- 1 class period

Materials Needed

- Student Activity Sheet 9A
- pencils or pens

Lesson Plan

1. PREPARE

Before class you should . . .
- review the lesson materials.

Before class students should . . .
- complete Student Activity Sheet 9A as preparatory homework.

2. TEACH

Focus

Begin by drawing a Venn diagram on the board. Explain to students that a Venn diagram is a way to show what is the same and different about two subjects. Things that are the same are listed in the overlapping area of the two circles. Things that describe only one subject are listed in the separate areas of each circle.

Guide

- Label one circle "Turn of First Millennium" and the other "Turn of Second Millennium."
- Challenge students to list at least two similarities between the two changes of the millennia and five unique items for each change.
- Next, focus students' attention on the difference in both the number of people and the percentage of the total population aware of the change in each millennium.
- Emphasize the relatively small number of people aware of the first millennium by conducting this activity: Draw a large circle on the board and label it "A.D. 2000: 6 billion people." Next to it, draw a circle about one sixth that size. Label it "A.D. 1000: 1 billion people."
- Treat this smaller circle as a pie graph. Shade all but about one eighth of the circle. Explain that what isn't shaded represents the European population at the turn of the first millennium. Shade about half of the remaining unshaded portion, explaining that what is left now represents roughly the number of people who were aware of the turn of the first millennium. Finally, shade all but a small sliver of the graph, explaining that what remains represents the number of

people who experienced the turn of the millennium as a shared event. Conclude by pointing out that, at most, the number of people who underwent the turn of the first millennium at the same time numbered in the thousands.

- Treat the larger circle in a similar way. Point out that no one can know how many people will participate in the turn of the second millennium as a shared event, but one estimate puts the number at a stunning 2 billion people. To reflect this estimate, shade two thirds of the circle.

- Lead students in a brief discussion to compare and contrast the number of people experiencing each turn of the millennium.

- Point out that experts agree that the turn of the millennium will be the most widely recognized and celebrated event in human history.

Close

- Conclude by reminding students of the geographic differences between the two turns of the millennia. Whereas the first was only recognized in Europe, the second will be celebrated on every continent.

3. EVALUATE

- **Formal Evaluation** Collect and examine individual students' work on Student Activity Sheet 9A.

- **Informal Evaluation** Observe individual students' attitudes and contributions during the group discussion period.

- **Self-Evaluation** Have students consider these questions: What are three new things I learned from this lesson? and What could I have done to make a better contribution to the class discussion?

4. EXTENSION AND ENRICHMENT

- Invite students to color world outline maps to indicate the difference in the geographic awareness of the turns of the first millennium and second millennium.

- Allow interested students to research and report to you on the Christian view of the first turn of the millennium.

Teacher to Teacher You can focus on the different numbers of people who knew or cared about the millennium and where they lived, as the lesson suggests. I would actually focus students' attention on how the first millennium was really a Christian event, whereas this one is much more secular.

Journal Activities

You may wish to assign the self-evaluation questions as journal topics. As an alternative, challenge students to explore further these questions: What would I have liked about living in A.D. 1000? What would I not like?

Name _____

Date _____

It's Happened Before

The millennium has turned once before. About 1,000 years ago, people marked the change from the first millennium to the second millennium. We're about to mark the change from the second millennium to the third millennium.

Are there any lessons we can learn from the first change of the millennium? If so, what are they?

Focus | The following essay considers these and other questions. Read the essay, and then answer the questions that follow.

It's Happened Before

As we approach the upcoming turn of the millennium, we naturally think about the last turn of the millennium. And one thing is clear: The last turn of the millennium was very much the same—and very much different—from the one we face.

It's the Same . . .

One similarity stands out. Most people will celebrate the turn of the millennium at the end of 1999, even though the millennium doesn't technically end until the end of the year 2000. The same thing happened last time: People marked the end of the millennium in 999, instead of waiting until it really ended, at the end of the year 1000.

Another similarity is that people view it as a special moment in history. Just as people today view the turn of the millennium as a rare and important event, people 1,000 years ago thought that the new millennium marked something of important consequence.

. . . But Different

But that's about where the similarities end.

A huge difference is the number of people who are aware of the turn of the millennium. Today, millions or even billions of the 6 billion people on earth are aware of the turn of the millennium. One thousand years ago, there were only about 1 billion people on earth. And only a tiny percentage of them were aware of the turn of the millennium.

Today, most people live under the same calendar— the Gregorian calendar—on which we'll mark the turn of the millennium. One thousand years ago, the Gregorian calendar hadn't even been invented. People used its predecessor, the Julian calendar, which dated back to Roman times. And it was only in Christian areas (chiefly Europe) that the Julian calendar was being used at all. So the turn of the first millennium to the second millennium was marked only in one corner of the world.

(continued)

                   Millennium: An Interdisciplinary Investigation

It's Happened Before (continued)

But not even all of Europe thought about the turn of the millennium. Only a small percentage of the people then were educated well enough to know when the date was. Moreover, different versions of the calendar were used in different parts of Europe.

So while the turn of the millennium is a worldwide event today, 1,000 years ago it was marked in just one part of the world (Europe), by a small percentage of people, and on different days.

Those who marked the turn of the millennium viewed it, as we said, as a special day. For them, though, it was viewed totally within the context of the Christian tradition. Many saw it as heralding the end of the world, or the Second Coming of Jesus Christ to Earth. The turn of the millennium was viewed with great fear and hope. Crowds gathered at churches, and many people saw signs and omens that the end of the world was at hand. It is reported that many people died of fright. When the fateful moment passed, and the world had not ended, many took it as a great blessing, wept with joy, and felt the world had been reborn.

Today, there are many Christians who view the second millennium with the same reverence and awe. But they do so in a world where the turn of the millennium is more widely recognized, and not viewed entirely as a religious event.

1. What are two ways in which the upcoming turn of the millennium is similar to the one of a thousand years ago?

2. How are the number of people aware of the turn of the millennium today greater both in terms of *number* and *percentage* than the number of people aware of it 1,000 years ago?

3. How is the upcoming turn of the millennium different *geographically* from the first turn of the millennium?

4. How did the people who were aware of the first turn of the millennium view it differently from the way many people do today?

LESSON 10: Past Predictions About the Year 2000

Student Activity Sheet Disciplines and Levels

Student Activity Sheet	Discipline(s)	Level(s)
10A	social studies	A, B, C

Lesson Snapshot

In this lighthearted lesson, students read and respond to past predictions about what life would be like in the year 2000.

Objectives

- Students will examine past predictions about life in the year 2000.

- Students will appreciate the year 2000 as a benchmark date.

- Students will analyze the reasons people attempt to predict the future and the factors that influence their predictions.

- Students will apply the following critical thinking skills: application, analysis, synthesis, and evaluation.

Class Time Required

- One half class period

Materials Needed

- Student Activity Sheet 10A
- pencils or pens

Lesson Plan

1. PREPARE

Before class you should . . .

- review the lesson materials;

- decide whether you want students to complete the activity individually, with partners, in groups, or as a whole-class activity.

2. TEACH

Focus

- Open the lesson by inviting students to share any images of "the future" they've encountered in books, on television, or in the movies. Record salient ones on the board. Use their examples as a springboard for a discussion about visions people have of the future.

- Explain to students that the year 2000 has long stood as a benchmark date for predicting the future, and challenge them to explain why this is so.

- Tell students that in this lesson they will have a chance to consider predictions about life in the year 2000 that were made when the year 2000 was still far in the future.

Guide

- Distribute one copy of Student Activity Sheet 10A to each student.

- You may choose to have students complete the activity individually, with partners, or in small groups. The activity also works very well as a whole-class activity.

- As students complete the activity, focus their attention on the thinking behind question 4. Guide students into seeing how the present colors people's views of the future.

Close

- Conclude by having students discuss their answers to question 2 on the activity sheet.

3. EVALUATE

- **Formal Evaluation** If students worked independently, collect and examine individual students' work on Student Activity Sheet 10A.

- **Informal Evaluation** Observe individual students' attitudes and contributions during the group or class work period.
- **Self-Evaluation** Have students consider these questions: Why is it important to compare life today with what people in the past thought it would be like? and Did I find this activity enjoyable? Why or why not?

4. EXTENSION AND ENRICHMENT

- Encourage students to investigate and evaluate the predictions of famous figures such as Nostradamus.
- Encourage students to make their own forecasts of life in the future, and provide the rationale behind each prediction.

Teacher to Teacher   This activity should be fun, so work to keep it that way. Let the students laugh at some of the sillier predictions. Help them see, though, why they didn't seem silly at the time they were made.

Journal Activities

You may wish to assign the self-evaluation questions as journal topics. As an alternative, challenge students to further explore this question: Why do people feel the need to try to predict the future?

Rocket Cars and Domed Cities

The year 2000 has loomed as something special for generations—even centuries. In the past, people have tried to predict what life would be like in this special year.

Focus

> In the box below are 21 predictions that people in the past have made about life in the year 2000. Read each one, and think about whether it has come true. Also, think about *why* people of the past thought that life in the future would be that way. Then answer the questions that follow.

In the Year 2000 . . .

21 predictions about the dawn of the 21st century

- Video phones—telephones with television attachments—will have replaced traditional telephones.

- Medium and large cities will be covered with giant clear domes, under which the climate will be perfectly controlled.

- We will have a cure for the common cold.

- Cancer will be easily treated and cured with pills.

- Machines will replace defective body organs.

- Rocket vehicles will have replaced cars.

- Helicopters will have replaced cars.

- Bicycles will have replaced cars.

- Hovercraft will have replaced cars.

- Schools will not be divided into grades.

- Schools will be open 24 hours a day, with people of all ages attending classes.

- No one will want to live in a very large house.

- Evidence of life will be found on the moon.

- The world will have been destroyed by nuclear war.

- Robots will do the work of firefighters (and police officers, and nurses, and surgeons, and truck drivers, and . . .).

- People will no longer have lawns.

- Arts will be more popular than sports.

- People will take pills instead of sleeping.

- People will take pleasure trips to Mars.

- The world will be run by a giant computer buried deep below the earth's crust.

- An earthquake will cause most of North America to be covered by a sea.

(continued)

Rocket Cars and Domed Cities (continued)

1. Have any of these predictions come true?

2. Why is it so difficult to accurately predict the future?

3. Have you read or seen any other predictions about life in the year 2000 (perhaps in a science fiction story or movie)? If so, add them to the list.

4. The helicopter was developed in the 1940's and proved its value in many ways during the 1950's. The prediction about helicopters replacing cars was made during this time. What technology is so impressive to people today that they might think it will alter the world in the future?

5. For generations, predictions about the future typically focused on the year 2000. Why do you think this is so?

Unit III

An Event of a Lifetime:

THE MILLENNIUM TURNS

LESSON 11: Everyone's Talking About It

Student Activity Sheet Disciplines and Levels

Student Activity Sheet	Discipline(s)	Level(s)
11A	social studies; computer science; language arts	B, C
11B	social studies	A, B, C
11C	social studies; language arts	A, B, C

Lesson Snapshot

The purpose of this lesson is to give students the opportunity to measure the amount of attention being given the turn of the millennium in the media, in the marketplace, and by individuals. To this end, they use databases to conduct keyword searches using terms related to the turn of the millennium, go on a millennium scavenger hunt in the media and the marketplace, and interview people about their awareness and reactions to the turn of the millennium.

Objectives

- Students will use computers to locate information about the turn of the millennium and related topics.
- Students will employ newspapers, magazines, and other media to search for evidence of the importance being given the turn of the millennium.
- Students will conduct interviews.
- Students will apply the following critical thinking skills: application, analysis, synthesis, and evaluation.

Class Time Required

- 2–3 class periods

Materials Needed

- Student Activity Sheets 11A, 11B, and 11C
- pencils or pens

Lesson Plan

1. PREPARE

Before class you should . . .

- review the lesson materials;
- locate appropriate databases for students to search;
- consider which students you would like to have work together as partners.

2. TEACH

Focus

- Ask students how they know if something that happens at school is "a big deal" or an important event.
- Guide them into understanding that such events cause people to talk about them a great deal; people say that "everyone's talking about it" or something similar. Elicit examples from students.
- Explain that larger groups of people function the same way as the students at school. At the community, country, and even world level, important events are talked about by "everyone" (or large numbers of people, anyway). Often this "talking" is done in newspaper and magazine articles, books, and other forms of communication.
- Point out that the turn of the millennium is something that "everyone is talking about," and in this lesson they'll use some fun techniques to see just how true this is.

Guide

- Challenge students to explain why database search results are a good measure of how important a topic is to people. Encourage them to see how topics of greater concern generally have more written about them, and that these higher numbers of written references are reflected in database search results.

- Depending on your students' experience, you may need to review or explain the nature of databases and database search techniques. Tailor your explanation to the databases available to students.

- You may wish to take the class as a whole to the location of the computer terminals and use Student Activity Sheet 11A as a class project.

- The scavenger hunt on Student Activity Sheet 11B is self-explanatory. You may wish to complete it yourself first, so that you can give hints to students if they have difficulty locating specific items.

- Student Activity Sheet 11C guides students in interviewing an adult about the turn of the millennium. Consider reviewing students' questions with them individually before they conduct their interviews. You might also wish to model an interview for the class.

Close

- Ensure that students understand the important role that database searching will play for

them throughout their school careers and beyond.

- Consider rewarding the winners of the scavenger hunt with some sort of prize.

- Invite students to describe their interviews orally to the rest of the class. Close by guiding the class in drawing general conclusions about what they have learned from the various interviews.

- Reemphasize the importance of the turn of the millennium, as evidenced by its presence in the media, the marketplace, and the minds of individuals.

3. EVALUATE

- **Formal Evaluation** Collect and examine individual students' work on Student Activity Sheets 11A and 11C.

- **Informal Evaluation** Observe individual students' attitudes and contributions during the group or partner work period.

- **Self-Evaluation** Have students consider these questions: Why is it important that I know how to locate information using a computer? and What did I do well during my interview? What could I have done better?

4. EXTENSION AND ENRICHMENT

- Encourage students to conduct additional interviews.

- Allow students to use computers to research one particular aspect of the turn of the millennium and report what they find to the class.

Teacher to Teacher You should use Student Activity Sheet 11A as an opportunity for students to use search engines on the Internet. My students hear a lot about the Internet, but the more they use it the more familiar they are with it. They should also know how to use the electronic card catalog. These skills are vital.

The scavenger hunt is more fun in teams of two or three students each.

Journal Activities

You may wish to assign the self-evaluation questions as journal topics. As an alternative, challenge students to explore further this question: Why is the amount of information written about a topic a good measure of how important that topic is to people?

A Keyword Search

The turn of the millennium is literally something that happens only once in a thousand years. Because it is such a rare event, it is very much on the minds of people all over the world.

Want proof? Just enter *millennium* as a keyword on any library computer. A *keyword* is a single word that serves as the key to a topic. Most topics have more than one keyword. For example, if your topic is ballet, your keywords might be *ballerina, ballet,* and *dance.*

The computer takes whatever keyword is entered and searches its database for matches. If you enter the keyword *millennium* in a library's computer card catalog, the computer will search its database of book titles in the library. It will then display all of the titles of books in the library that include the word millennium.

Of course, there are other databases you can search besides electronic card catalogs. For example, there are special magazine and newspaper databases. There are databases of company names, and even of consumer products. Many databases not only match your keywords to

titles, but also to such things as subject areas and words in the actual text of the article.

Perhaps the biggest database of all is the Internet, a worldwide network of computers. The key to finding what you want on the Internet is to use special computer programs that will search the Internet for you. These programs are called search engines.

Search engines work like the index of a book. In a book index, you locate the topic you want to read about and then turn to the pages indicated. On the Internet, you enter the topic you're interested in (in the form of a keyword) and the search engine searches through the Internet for you, listing all of the Internet sites that have information about your topic.

Whether you search library databases, specialized databases, or the Internet, the key to finding what you want is to use the right keywords.

Focus

> In this lesson, you will identify keywords you can use to search computers for information about the turn of the millennium. Complete each of the following steps.

Step 1: Identify keywords.

In the following box, list as many possible keywords as you can that are associated with the upcoming turn of the millennium. Don't limit yourself. *Millennium* is an obvious choice. But other good choices are *2000, 2001, century,* and so on. List as many as you can.

(continued)

A Keyword Search *(continued)*

Step 2: Identify key phrases.

Some computers will search the actual text of magazine or newspaper articles. If this is the case, you can also search for phrases in the article. These are called key phrases. What key phrases might you search for to find information about the turn of the millennium as we approach the end of the century? (Hint: There are two key phrases in the previous sentence.)

Step 3: Try out your keywords and key phrases.

Choose five of the keywords and key phrases you identified in Steps 1 and 2 to try out. Go to the public library and try them on as many databases as you can (library card catalogs, news-paper databases, the Internet, and so on). As you work at the computer, complete the follow-ing chart.

MILLENNIUM COMPUTER SEARCH	
Date: _____	
Computer or database used: _____	
Keyword or Key Phrase	**Number of Listings**

(continued)

A Keyword Search (continued)

Step 4: Evaluate your search results.

It is important to review your search results to see which key words and phrases were most helpful to you.

1. Which keyword gave you the most listings?

2. Which key phrases gave you the most listings?

3. Which keyword or key phrases gave you the most *relevant* listings?

4. Overall, did you get many or few listings on the general topic of the turn of the millennium?

5. What can you conclude from your answer to question 4?

A Millennium Scavenger Hunt

Have you ever gone on a scavenger hunt? If so, you know that the winner is the person or team who can find all of the things on the list first.

How about a millennium scavenger hunt? It's just like a regular scavenger hunt, except you don't need to actually get each item on the list. (You just need to see it and tell where you've seen it.)

Focus | The winner of the scavenger hunt is the person or team who can find every item on the following list. To prove you've found each one, write down where you found it, saw it, or heard about it. Ready, set, go!

MILLENNIUM SCAVENGER HUNT	
Item to Find	**Where Found**
1. a product named "millennium," or "2000," or something similar	
2. a TV or radio commercial or a print ad that refers to the turn of the millennium	
3. an article in a newspaper or magazine that refers to "the 21st century"	
4. an article in a newspaper or magazine that includes a phrase similar to "As we approach the end of the millennium . . ."	
5. a book with the date "2000" or "2001" in the title	
6. a public project with "2000," "2001," "21st century," or "millennium" in its name	
7. a television show, radio show, or movie about the turn of the millennium	
8. a magazine article about the turn of the millennium	
9. a newspaper article about the turn of the millennium	

Conducting an Interview

The turn of the millennium is a very big deal. Around the world, people are thinking about it and planning for what promises to be the biggest celebration in human history.

But what do the people in your community think about the turn of the millennium? Are they excited about it, or is it not a very big deal to them? Are they looking at it as a time to think about the past, or a time to plan for the future? The only way to find out is to ask them.

Focus | In this lesson, you will conduct an interview to find out how someone in your community feels about the turn of the millennium. Carefully follow the steps below.

1. Decide whom to interview.

Who will you interview? You may choose to interview any responsible person. Everyone is unique and will have individual views on the turn of the millennium. Keep in mind, however, that some people might have a special interest in the event. For example, a community official might be able to talk about community plans to celebrate the event. An artist might talk about how artwork might be affected by the turn of the millennium.

In the following space, write the names of several people whom you might like to interview.

Possible Interview Subjects

2. Decide on the purpose of your interview.

Are you going to interview someone to find out how that person feels personally about the turn of the millennium? Or might you interview someone in a particular job to find out how the turn of the millennium might affect his or her profession? The purpose of your interview might depend on whom you interview. But it is also up to you to focus on the information you'd like most to know.

(continued)

       Millennium: An Interdisciplinary Investigation

Conducting an Interview *(continued)*

In the following space, identify the purpose of your interview.

Purpose of Interview

---

3. *Plan your interview.*

Planning is key to conducting a successful interview. You don't want to go in "cold," not prepared to ask questions. So you should identify at least five questions to ask the person you will interview. Try to write open-ended questions—the kind that require more than a "yes" or "no" answer. That way the person you are interviewing will share more information with you.

In the space that follows, write at least five open-ended interview questions. Each question should be related to the purpose of the interview you identified in Step 2. Some questions have been suggested for you.

Interview Questions

Do you know what the turn of the millennium is?

Do you think it's an important event? Why or why not?

What does the turn of the millennium mean to you personally?

(continued)

Conducting an Interview *(continued)*

Interviewing Guidelines

- **Be polite.** The person you interview will respond more favorably if you are considerate. You will also enjoy the interview more. When you approach the person, clearly explain that you would like to interview her or him about the turn of the millennium for a school project. Tell the person how long you expect the interview to last, and arrange it for a convenient time. During the interview, be respectful: Do not interrupt, and don't ask offensive questions.

- **Be flexible.** Although you should ask the questions you plan to, be flexible if the person brings up something about the turn of the millennium you hadn't thought of. Listen carefully, and feel free to ask questions about this new topic.

- **Listen, listen, listen!** Any good reporter will tell you that the best interviews are the ones where the interviewer (you) talks a little, and listens a lot. Remember, the goal is to learn about the other person's thoughts and feelings, and to gain informa-

---

4. *Review some interviewing guidelines.*

The guidelines in the following box will help you conduct a successful interview. Read them carefully before you interview your subject, and follow them during the interview itself.

5. *Conduct your interview.*

Be sure to follow the Interviewing Guidelines as you do so.

6. *Learn from your interview.*

There is little point in conducting an interview unless you learn something from it. You can learn something from every interview, even if it isn't what you were expecting to. To help you learn from your interview, answer these questions after you have completed it.

- What was the most interesting thing the person you interviewed talked about?

- Did you learn something about the turn of the millennium you hadn't considered before? What was it?

- How do the person's thoughts about the turn of the millennium compare to your own?

LESSON 12: **When Does the Millennium** *Really* **Turn?**

Student Activity Sheet Disciplines and Levels

Student Activity Sheet	Discipline(s)	Level(s)
12A	social studies; mathematics	A, B, C
12B	social studies; mathematics	B, C
12C	social studies; mathematics; science	B, C

Lesson Snapshot

The millennium turns at the end of the year 2000, not at the end of 1999, as is commonly believed. In this lesson, students explore this fact through three means. First, they calculate the end of the millennium mathematically based on their knowledge of centuries and the Gregorian calendar. Second, they analyze the National Institute of Science and Technology's position on the question. Finally, they investigate the fact that the millennium will turn technically at 24 different times, as they learn about time zones and the international date line.

Objectives

- Students will apply mathematical skills and historical knowledge to calculate the actual date and time of the turn of the millennium.

- Students will analyze a government document concerned with the date the millennium turns.

- Students will explore how the existence of time zones and the international date line affect the turn of the millennium.

- Students will apply the following critical thinking skills: interpretation, application, analysis, and synthesis.

Class Time Required

- 2 class periods

Materials Needed

- Student Activity Sheets 12A, 12B, and 12C
- calculators (optional)
- pencils or pens

Lesson Plan

1. PREPARE

Before class you should . . .

- review the lesson materials;
- decide whether students should complete activity sheets individually or with partners.

2. TEACH

Focus

- Tell students that the class will hold a vote on when the millennium will turn. Elicit "candidate dates" from students (likely, "midnight, December 31, 1999" and "midnight, December 31, 2000") and write them on the board. Have students cast their votes by raising their hands. Tally the votes on the board.

- Tell students that they can check the validity of their election results by completing an activity sheet that will guide them in calculating specifically when the millennium actually turns.

75

Guide

- Distribute one copy of Student Activity Sheet 12A to each student.

- Work through the activity sheet as a class. Ask the questions aloud, and perform the calculations on the board.

- By the end of this exercise, students should conclude that the millennium actually turns at the end of the year 2000.

- Point out to students that this is technically true, but that those who voted for the end of the year 1999 as the turn date have support for their position.

- Distribute one copy of Student Activity Sheet 12B to each student. Again, work through the sheet as a class. Emphasize that the millennium actually has two turn dates: the popular date (end of 1999) and the technical date (end of the year 2000).

Close

- Explain that there are even more dates—and times—when the millennium turns.

- Distribute one copy of Student Activity Sheet 12C to each student to complete as homework.

- After they have completed the activity sheet, follow it up with an in-class demonstration. Use a flashlight and a rotating globe to point out how dawn—and a new day—reaches different parts of the earth at different times.

3. EVALUATE

- **Formal Evaluation** Collect and examine individual students' work on Student Activity Sheet 12C.

- **Informal Evaluation** Observe individual students' attitudes and contributions during the group discussion period. Occasionally, ask specific students to explain the nature and purpose of time zones and the international date line.

- **Self-Evaluation** Have students consider these questions: Is it easier for me to understand when the millennium turns by doing the math itself or by reading an explanation? and How can I make my home-study time more productive?

4. EXTENSION AND ENRICHMENT

- Have student volunteers make a chart of the dates and times in major foreign cities compared with the current date and time in their own community.

- Invite a student to make a presentation to the class on the history of time zones and the international date line, specifying when and by whom they were developed.

Teacher to Teacher   Students take pride in knowing—and even bragging—about when the millennium *really* ends, as opposed to when most people think it ends.

You might want to explain a little bit more about what the National Institute of Standards and Technology (NIST) actually is and does. Or, have a student do research and a short paper on NIST to present to you and the class.

Journal Activities

You may wish to assign the self-evaluation questions as journal topics. As an alternative, challenge students to explore further this question: Even people who know the end of the millennium isn't until the end of the year 2000 will still celebrate it at the end of the year 1999. Why?

Calculating the Beginning of the
Third Millennium

When does the next millennium start? Most people say that it begins the moment the year 2000 arrives. In other words, they say the second millennium ends and the third millennium begins at midnight, December 31, 1999.

But are they right? You might be surprised.

Focus | To find out when the millennium really turns, complete the following steps.

1. What was the number of the first year A.D.? (Hint: There was no year 0.)

2. How many years are there in a century?

3. Based on your answers to questions 1 and 2, what was the last year of the first century A.D.?

4. What year was the last year of the second century A.D.?

5. What year was the last year of the tenth century A.D. (which was also the end of the first millennium)?

6. What year was the last year of the fifteenth century A.D. (which was also the middle of the second millennium)?

7. What year will be the last year of the twentieth century A.D. (which will also be the end of the second millennium)?

8. When will the third millennium start?

9. There are 1,000 years in a millennium. Based on your answer to question 1, what year will be the last year in the second millennium?

10. Are you surprised by your answers to questions 8 and 9? Explain why or why not.

What Does NIST Say?

You may have never heard of NIST. But, in a way, this government agency regulates every second of your life—literally!

NIST stands for the National Institute of Standards and Technology. It is the federal government agency in charge of setting standards for measurement. Of the measurements it regulates is the measurement of time.

One of NIST's big concerns these days is answering questions about the turn of the millennium. A common one is "When will the new millennium begin?" In response, NIST has distributed an information sheet to the public.

Focus | The excerpt below was taken from a public information sheet put out by NIST. Read it. Then answer the questions that follow.

On What Date Will the 21st Century Begin?

This is a date that no organization, including NIST, has the authority to regulate. However, one logical answer to the question is that because there was never a year "zero," and a century must have 100 years, then each century must begin with a year numbered "1." [For example, 101, 201, 301, and so on.] In other words, the twentieth century should be considered [starting on January 1, 1901] and ending on December 31, 2000, and the twenty-first century as starting on January 1, 2001.

However, human nature being what it is, most of us will still opt to have that "once-in-a-century" New Year's Eve bash on December 31, 1999.

—*National Institute of Standards and Technology*

1. According to NIST, the date the twenty-first century will begin—the turn of the millennium— "is a date that no organization, including NIST, has the authority to regulate."

   a. Why do you think they say this?

   b. Do you agree with this position, or should there be an organization that *does* have such authority? Explain your answer.

(continued)

What Does NIST Say? *(continued)*

2. What "one logical answer" to the question of when the new millennium begins does NIST give?

> **National Institute of Standards and Technology.**
>
> **On What Date Will the 21st Century Begin?**
>
> This is a date that no organization, including NIST, has the authority to regulate. However, one logical answer to the question is that because there was never a year "zero," and a century must have 100 years, then each century must begin with a year numbered "1." (For example, 101, 201, 301, and so on.) In other words, the 20th century should be considered as starting on January 1, 1901 and ending on December 31, 1000, and the 2001.
>
> However, human nature being what it is, most of us will still opt to have that "once-in-a-century" New Years Eve bash on December 31, 1999."

3. In the second paragraph, NIST says that people will celebrate on December 31, 1999, because of "human nature." What do you think they mean by this?

4. One NIST official, when asked when the new millennium begins, said, "There are two answers to that question: the popular answer, and the technical answer."

   a. What do you think the "popular" answer is?

   b. Why do you think it's called the "popular" answer?

   c. What do you think the "technical" answer is?

   d. Why do you think it's called the "technical" answer?

5. When do *you* think the new millennium will start? Explain your answer.

Name _____

Date _____

When Does the Millennium *Really* Turn?
Student Activity Sheet 12C

When Will It Start for You?

The turn of the millennium is a worldwide event, to be sure. But equally as certain is the fact that the new millennium will not begin everywhere on earth at the same time.

How can this be?

Focus

> To find out, read the following article and study the accompanying map. Then use them to answer the questions that follow. Use the back of your paper if you need more room to write.

Time Zones and the International Date Line

It might surprise you to learn that it is never the same time all over the world. In fact, it isn't even ever the same *day* all over the world. Why? Because the world is divided into different time zones.

Time Zones

There are 24 time zones in the world, since the earth completes one rotation on its axis in 24 hours. Each time zone is as wide as the distance that the earth rotates in one hour. There is a one-hour difference between neighboring time zones. For example, when it is 2 P.M. in your time zone, it is only 1 P.M. in the time zone to your west, but already 3 P.M. in the time zone to your east.

Why do time zones exist? Time zones were created to clarify time relationships. If there were no time zones, every clock in the world would show the same time. At noon, for example, the sun would be rising in some places, and setting in others. It would be the middle of the day in one part of the world and the middle of the night in another. How confusing!

By dividing the earth into 24 time zones, noon in every part of the world is always about when the sun is at its highest point. Sunrise is in the middle A.M. hours, and sunset is in the middle P.M. hours. This helps avoid confusion. Travelers, businesses that work with people around the globe, and governments in different parts of the world can communicate more effectively since time is similar in all parts of the world.

Greenwich Mean Time

The base time zone is called Greenwich Mean Time, through which the prime meridian (0° longitude) runs. Traveling west from this time zone, the time becomes one hour earlier for each time zone you cross. Traveling east, the time becomes one hour later for each time zone you cross.

The International Date Line

Directly opposite the prime meridian, at 180° longitude, runs the International Date Line. The International Date Line marks the place where each new day on the calendar officially begins. The date to the west of the International Date Line is one day earlier than the date to the east of it.

How does this work? Imagine you travel west from the prime meridian, where it is Greenwich Mean Time. The time becomes one hour earlier for each time zone you cross. There are 12 time zones between the prime meridian and the International Date Line. So the time at the International Date Line is 12 hours *earlier* than Greenwich Mean Time. When it is noon at the prime meridian, it is still the *previous midnight* at the

(continued)

When Will It Start for You? *(continued)*

Now imagine you travel east from the prime meridian. Traveling this way, the time becomes one hour later for each time zone you cross. So the time at the International Date Line is 12 hours *later* than Greenwich Mean Time. When it is noon at the prime meridian, it is already the *following midnight* at the International Date Line.

How can the time be both 12 hours later and 12 hours earlier at the International Date Line? It depends on which side of the International Date Line you're on. If you're just to the west, it's the later midnight. If you're just to the east, it's the earlier one. So by crossing the date line, you change the date on the calendar. Traveling west across the line, you add a day. Traveling east, you subtract a day.

Each new date on the calendar starts just to the west of the International Date Line and moves westward around the earth as the earth spins. As the earth spins, the new day is marked—one hour later—in each time zone.

1. Why won't the start of the new millennium be celebrated at the same moment all over the world?

2. Explain why there will be 24 different moments at which the new millennium begins.

3. Where on earth will the new millennium begin first?

4. Explain how the earth's rotation is the reason that time zones and the international date line exist.

5. Some people are planning to celebrate the moment of the arrival of the new millennium at several different moments. How do you think they can accomplish this?

(continued)

When Will It Start for You? *(continued)*

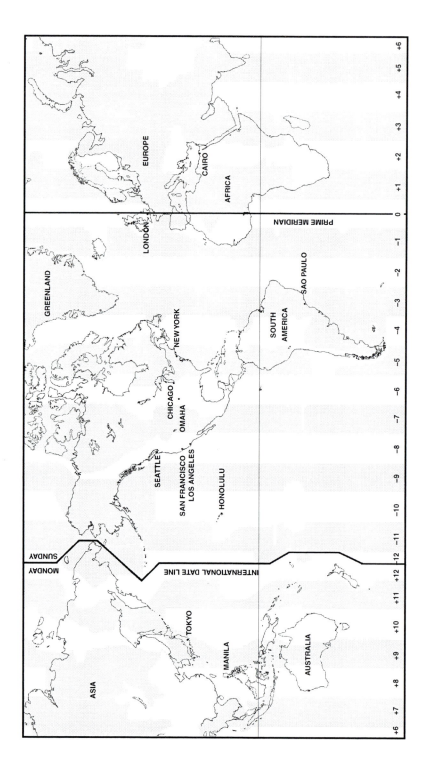

Millennium: An Interdisciplinary Investigation

LESSON 13: Computers and the Turn of the Millennium

Student Activity Sheet Disciplines And Levels

Student Activity Sheet	Discipline(s)	Level(s)
13A	social studies; mathematics; language arts	B, C
13B	computer science; mathematics; social studies	C

Lesson Snapshot

Students read and respond to a newspaper article that explains the nature and ramifications of the "Year 2000 Problem": the problem that computers around the world face as their software reads the date "00" as 1900 instead of 2000. They also follow a flowchart to program a computer to count down to the end of the second millennium and then count up into the third millennium.

Objectives

- Students will describe and analyze the problems computers and computer operators face with the date change from 1999 to 2000.
- Students will apply programming skills and techniques to create software that functions as a millennium countdown clock.
- Students will apply the following critical thinking skills: interpretation and application.

Class Time Required

- 2 class periods

Materials Needed

- Student Activity Sheets 13A and 13B
- pencils or pens
- computer loaded with BASIC or other programming language

Lesson Plan

1. PREPARE

Before class you should . . .

- review the lesson materials;
- arrange for student access to programmable computers.

Before class students should . . .

- complete Student Activity Sheet 13A as homework.

2. TEACH

Focus

- Challenge students to name as many examples of computers and computer uses as they can. As they call out examples, list them on the board. Try to elicit at least a dozen examples in many different aspects of life.
- Follow the same procedure to create a second list of computer users (businesses, individuals, the government, and so on).
- Tell students that virtually every single one of the hundreds of millions of computers on the planet will be affected by the Year 2000 Problem.

Guide

- Have a volunteer explain what the Year 2000 Problem is.
- Lead a brief discussion on why this can pose such a problem for people in all walks of life.

- Create a table on the board with the heading "The Year 2000 Problem" and these row titles: What, Where, When, Why, Who, and How.

- Guide the class in completing the table. Ask: What is the Year 2000 Problem? What is another name for the problem? Where are the computers affected by it located? When will this problem occur? When did this problem start? Why did this problem come about? Who will be affected by the problem? Who will fix it? How can it be fixed? and How much will it cost to fix?

- When the table is completed, make sure students have a rounded understanding of the problem, its effects, and its solution.

- The creation of the computer program described on Student Activity Sheet 13B will vary with your students' computer knowledge and access to computers.

Close

- Conclude by emphasizing the fundamental role that computers play in modern life, and how many benefits they provide. Point out, however, that our great reliance on these machines makes us especially vulnerable to any widespread problems they may have.

3. EVALUATE

- **Formal Evaluation** Collect and examine individual students' work on Student Activity Sheet 13A.

- **Informal Evaluation** Observe individual students' attitudes and contributions during the group discussion period. Monitor students during the creation of the computer program.

- **Self-Evaluation** Have students consider these questions: How can I use a pen to help me learn and remember important points when I read newspaper articles? and What did I like the most and least about this assignment?

4. EXTENSION AND ENRICHMENT

- Challenge a group of students to conduct research to find out how your school or your school district is addressing the Year 2000 Problem, and to report what they learn to the class.

Teacher to Teacher   Doing the computer program really depends on the class. But the newspaper article is a good chance to remind them how important computers are and how they affect everybody.

Journal Activities

You may wish to assign the self-evaluation questions as journal topics. As an alternative, challenge students to explore further this question: How did computers affect my life this week?

The Year 2000 Problem

How many different ways do computers touch your life? The answer is *a lot.*

From keeping track of your grades at school to helping weather forecasters know whether to recommend that you wear a coat to school, from running appliances in the cafeteria to scheduling the bus that takes you home, computers affect your life every day in many ways.

In fact, they affect billions of people's lives around the world. Computers are a fundamental part of life on earth at the end of the second millennium.

Unfortunately, the end of the second millennium itself presents a huge problem for virtually every computer on the planet. No matter how "intelligent" they are, no matter how much memory they have, and no matter how powerful they are, computers just can't handle the change from 1999 to 2000. Why not? Because they've got a "Year 2000 Problem."

Computer problem for the year 2000

by J.P. Conners

Focus | The following newspaper article explains what the Year 2000 Problem is and what it means for you and for millions of other people. Read the article. Then answer the questions that follow. Use the back of your paper if you need more room to write.

The Year 2000 Problem

If you use a computer, you could go to sleep after celebrating New Year's Eve in 1999 and wake up a victim of what has come to be called the "Year 2000 Problem."

Even if you don't work directly with computers, you will certainly feel the problem's effects—and will certainly help pay for a solution. Published reports say companies, governments and other organizations could spend a whopping $600 billion to fix the Year 2000 Problem during the final years of this century.

So, what's the problem?

When nearly every computer around reads or writes a date, it just uses the last two digits for the year. Thus, 98 becomes 1998, 75 is 1975, 88 is 1988 and so on.

Those same computers see 00 as 1900, and that's at the heart of this timely foul-up. A file or program could refer to the year 2000, but the computer will think it's dealing with a time before the Wright brothers invented the airplane.

That will, at best, cause confusion and errors. At worst, it could shut down whole systems confused by what appears to be a date before any others in its database.

Finding and fixing what some call the "Millennium Bug" on any one computer or program isn't too tough. It's just a matter of rewriting a few lines of computer code. But it becomes very tough when you consider the scope of this problem. Virtually every aspect of our lives is touched upon, in one way or another, by computers. Banks, ATM's and credit card companies use them to keep track of our money and purchases. Airline pilots are told where and when to fly, what or who is supposed to be aboard, and whether the weather is good or bad by a glance at some computer's glowing face. Grocery stores use them to order everything from soup to nuts, and keep tabs on when the milk will sour. Everything from the space shuttle to your thermostat relies on computers.

Finding and solving the Year 2000 Problem in all those computers and software is a daunting—and expensive—task. Researchers estimate the cost will be from $300 billion to $600 billion worldwide. The price tag for the federal government alone will be around $30 billion.

How did we get into this mess?

(continued)

The Year 2000 Problem *(continued)*

For more than four decades, industry and businesses have written their computer programs with dates represented by only a two-digit year—for example, 95 versus 1995.

Doing it that way saved a bit—actually, two bytes—of storage space on computers every time the date was written. Back in the 1960's every little byte helped, and virtually all programmers used the two-digit year.

Later on, storage space wasn't as much of a concern, but no one changed the practice of writing computer code that used the two-digit year. Besides, at the rate technology was advancing, it was thought most computers would be replaced by the year 2000.

But frugal companies saved what they could of old computers as new ones came on-line, and merged old data files and software with new, regardless of whether programmers warned them that change was needed or not. In other words, the bug has been passed down from generation to generation of computers.

And treatment can't be put off any longer.

Many companies have mobilized resources and are offering services to help the millions and millions of computer users have a happy New Year, come the new millennium. But for the most part, such help comes with its own price tag, and some observers believe far too much has already been made of the Year 2000 Problem. They point to the huge sums computer consultants and businesses stand to make by fixing a problem that is, after all, of their own devising.

Still others believe we're underestimating the problem's potential impact on the pocketbook and on society.

Either way, it will cost less to fix the Year 2000 Problem than ignore it.

1. (a) Describe the Year 2000 Problem.

   (b) What else is the Year 2000 Problem being called?

2. Why is the Year 2000 Problem such a far-reaching problem?

3. Why did the Year 2000 Problem come about?

4. About how much will it cost to fix this problem?

5. Why did computer programmers of the past think that this problem would not develop?

3, 2, 1 . . . Happy New Year!

The most exciting time of any New Year's Eve is the final countdown to the end of the year—and the beginning of the new one.

This excitement will reach a fever pitch on December 31, 1999, as millions of people count down to the end of a year, a decade, a century, and a millennium all at once. But you don't have to wait until the final seconds to begin your countdown. With the help of a computer, you can begin your countdown today.

Focus | The flowchart at the right shows how a computer program can be written in the BASIC language (or another) to count down to midnight, December 31, 1999. Follow the flowchart to write your own program to make your computer a countdown machine.

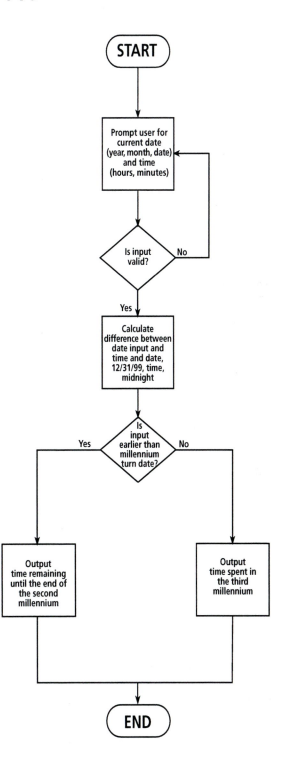

LESSON 14: **Finding Meaning in the Millennium**

Student Activity Sheet Disciplines and Levels

Student Activity Sheet	Discipline(s)	Level(s)
14A	social studies; language arts	B, C
14B	social studies	A, B, C

Lesson Snapshot

In the first activity sheet, students read and respond to leading thinkers' comments about why the turn of the millennium is viewed as such an important event. Through the second activity sheet, students explore the millennium as an economic event: a major public occurrence that has spawned countless consumer products, advertising schemes, and other economic ventures.

Objectives

- Students will analyze the comments of leading thinkers about the turn of the millennium.

- Students will investigate the economic repercussions of the turn of the millennium.

- Students will apply the following critical thinking skills: interpretation, analysis, and evaluation.

Class Time Required

- 2 class periods

Materials Needed

- Student Activity Sheets 14A and 14B
- pencils or pens

Lesson Plan

1. PREPARE

Before class you should . . .

- review the lesson materials.

Before class students should . . .

- complete Student Activity Sheet 14A as preparatory homework (optional);

- complete Student Activity Sheet 14B as preparatory homework.

2. TEACH

Focus

- If students haven't completed it as homework, distribute one copy of Student Activity Sheet 14A to each student.

- Explain that the activity sheet is essentially a group of quotations about why people are making so much of the turn of the millennium.

- Ask the class to explain why it is useful to review leading thinkers' comments about this major event.

Guide

- Work through each quotation with the class. Call on individuals to read each one aloud, then focus on the literal meaning of each quotation. Ensure that students understand difficult vocabulary words.

- Using the questions on the activity sheet as a guide, explore the message of each quotation. Find out if the class agrees or disagrees with each, and why.

- Conclude by having the class vote on the quotation that they think best answers the question of why the turn of the millennium is considered to be so important to people.

- Student Activity Sheet 14B exposes students to the many different ways that people are hoping to make money off the turn of the millennium. Invite volunteers to share their thoughts on what they read—which schemes seem most profitable, which seem silly, which would interest students, and so on.

Close

- Conclude by having students compare and contrast the very serious tone of the quotations with the rather frivolous nature of many of the moneymaking schemes.

- Emphasize that these differences testify to the widely different ways in which people respond to and find meaning in the turn of the millennium.

3. EVALUATE

- **Formal Evaluation** Collect and examine individual students' work on Student Activity Sheets 14A and 14B.

- **Informal Evaluation** Observe individual students' attitudes and contributions during the group discussion period. Notice which students respond more willingly to the serious discussion about the turn of the millennium and the more lighthearted discussion about its economic effects.

- **Self-Evaluation** Have students consider these questions: What could I have done to better understand each quotation? and How can I apply what I have learned to my own view of the meaning of the turn of the millennium?

4. EXTENSION AND ENRICHMENT

- Invite students to report to the class any new millennium-related product or advertisement they see.

- Challenge the class to conceive and develop their own millennium-related product.

Teacher to Teacher   These quotations are tough sledding. I would recommend that you either assign them to only the most advanced students or work through them sentence by sentence in class.

Why not have kids make their own millennium product? It would be a good opportunity for team-building and critical thinking and a chance for them to understand how the economy works firsthand.

Journal Activities

You may wish to assign the self-evaluation questions as journal topics. As an alternative, challenge students to explore further this question: How important do I think the turn of the millennium is?

Why Is It So Important to So Many?

Hundreds of millions of people find special meaning in the turn of the millennium. Why? What makes it such a special event to people?

Focus | Five leading thinkers have shed some light on why the turn of the millennium is viewed as such an important event. Read each of the following quotations carefully. Then answer the questions that follow; they are designed to help you understand what each quotation means. Use the back of your paper if you need more room.

Deep superstitions are tapped by rites that end one stage of life and launch another. We witness this every year as people make New Year's resolutions, impressed by the passage of time, apprehensive about the use of what is left to them. . . . The magic is bound to be more powerful when a year is ending along with a day. And these feel-ings are heightened further when a decade is ending, or a century. At the stroke of midnight 1999, a day, decade, a century, and a millennium will draw to a simultaneous, dramatic close.

—*Garry Wills*
author

Why does the author say people make New Year's resolutions?

What makes the stroke of midnight 1999 "dramatic"?

There is a natural tendency to think of one's own time as the hinge of history.
—*Evelyn Waugh*
author

Explain this statement in your own words.

Explain why you agree or disagree with the author's statement. If you agree, explain why you think there is a "natural tendency" to view one's own time this way.

This statement was not written with the turn of the millennium in mind. However, how might it apply to the turn of the millennium?

(continued)

Why Is It So Important to So Many? *(continued)*

> [The year 2000] bears the . . . weight of thousands of [postponed] hopes and unfulfilled predictions.
>
> —*Hillel Schwartz*
> *author and historian*

What "[postponed] hopes" might the author be referring to?

What do you think he means by "unfulfilled predictions"?

> The habit of thinking in terms of decades and centuries induces a self-fulfilling delusion, and the way people behave—or, at least, perceive their behavior—really does tend to change accordingly. Decades and centuries are like the clock cases inside which the pendulum of history swings. Strictly speaking, a new millennium begins every moment of every day; yet the approach of the year 2000 makes the present a peculiarly—indeed, a uniquely—good time for taking stock of our last thousand years of history, asking where they have led us and wondering where we go from here.
>
> —*Felipe Fernandez-Armesto*

What does the author mean by saying that "decades and centuries are like the clock cases inside which the pendulum of history swings"?

How is it that "a new millennium begins every moment of every day"?

What does the author think the approach of the year 2000 makes it a good time to do?

(continued)

Why Is It So Important to So Many? *(continued)*

> The millennium looms as civilization's most spectacular birthday. . . . Time is history's . . . framework—the way to make sense out of beginnings, middles, and ends. Everyone is born, and dies, in the middle of history's larger story. The millennium is a chance (the rarest) to see, or to imagine that we see, the greater human story. . . . Envisioning the end of one era and the beginning of another somehow infuses life with narrative meaning.
>
> —*Lance Morrow*
> *writer*

What does the millennium give us "a chance to see"?

What does the author mean by the statement "Time is history's . . . framework"?

Now it's your turn. Based on the quotations you just read and your own thoughts, answer this question: Why is the turn of the millennium so important to so many people?

Name _____

Date _____

The Millennium As an Economic Event

It's no secret: Americans, perhaps more than any other people, are famous for finding ways to make money from nearly any event. So it should come as no surprise that the turn of the millennium, the greatest celebration in history, is also one of the greatest money-making opportunities in American history.

What may surprise you, though, is just how much money there is to be made: The turn of the millennium—which is, after all, just a calendar date—has become a multibillion dollar industry.

Also surprising is the sheer number of different ways Americans have found to capitalize on the world's most spectacular birthday.

Focus | Listed on this page and the next are some of the hundreds of ways people hope to make money from the turn of the millennium. As you read, think about exactly how each venture could make money for the businesspeople involved. Then answer the questions that follow. Use the back of your paper if you need more room to write.

How the Turn of the Millennium Is Being Used to Make Money

In the Marketplace

- From skin care products to pots and pans, dozens of products bear the name "Millennium." (Many are misspelled, as "Milenium.")

- An American favorite—the T-shirt—is being printed in hundreds of different "millennial" ways, from "I lived through the turn of the millennium and all I got was this lousy T-shirt!" to shirts bearing the dates and logos of special millennium trips and celebrations.

- Souvenirs—key chains, stuffed animals, pens, and so on—are being made and sold by the millions to people who want to keep a reminder of the turn of the millennium.

- Several companies are coming out with their own "2000 Series" of their products. There is a 2000 Series of car stereos, for example, and a 2000 Series of jewelry.

- Food manufacturers are getting in on the act with "commemorative" flavored coffees, cookies, chips, soft drinks, and dozens of other products that are specially made or packaged to link them to the turn of the millennium.

- At least one company has created millennium trading cards, featuring important people of the second millennium.

- These are just a few examples: Business analysts consistently say that the turn of the millennium will spawn *thousands* of new products.

In the Media

- There are dozens of end-of-century and end-of-millennium documentary films that review the past and speculate about the future.

- More than one television show includes the word "millennium" in its title. Even writers for situation comedies have used the turn of the millennium as a basis for characters' jokes.

- Since the 1980's, magazines have run hundreds of stories about the turn of the millennium, many of them cover stories.

- Dozens of new books based on the turn of the millennium have been published. They include histories of the second millennium, forecasts for the third millennium, and everything in between.

(continued)

The Millennium As an Economic Event *(continued)*

- On the Internet, individuals, businesses, and other groups have set up a variety of sites that address all aspects of the turn of the millennium.

In the Travel and Entertainment Industry

- The people who make money from celebrations—caterers, party-planners, tuxedo-rental companies, and so on—are reporting record sales.

- The travel industry is benefiting in a big way, as it sells and people buy millennium theme trips and vacations.

In Advertising

- Phone companies report a run on customized phone numbers whose last four digits are 1999, 2000, and 2001.

- Next time you go to the mall, notice how many items are priced at $19.99. It's not a coincidence.

- Notice also how many advertisements include phrases like "Plan for the new century . . . (with our services)" and "Enter the new millennium with . . . (our product)."

1. Which of the moneymaking methods in the box do you think will be the most profitable? Why?

2. Why do you think companies think customers will buy products named "millennium"?

3. Do you find any of the products to be in poor taste? Explain your answer.

4. Which of the items described in the box do you think will have lasting value? Why?

5. Would you purchase any of the items described in the box? Why?

6. What other moneymaking schemes related to the turn of the millennium have you seen in your own life?

LESSON 15: Millennial Art: Creations for a Once-in-a-Lifetime Event

Student Activity Sheet Disciplines and Levels

Student Activity Sheet	Discipline(s)	Level(s)
15A	social studies; art	A, B, C
15B	social studies; art	A, B, C

Lesson Snapshot

Like other major events in history, the turn of the millennium will be celebrated and commemorated through artwork. In this lesson, students read about planned artworks, respond to them, and then simulate the role of artists and arts committee members to plan artwork for their own community.

Objectives

- Students will interpret and evaluate works of art planned to commemorate the turn of the millennium.
- Students will conceive and evaluate similar works of art.
- Students will simulate the role of a government committee.
- Students will apply the following critical thinking skills: interpretation, application, analysis, synthesis, and evaluation.

Class Time Required

- 2 class periods

Materials Needed

- Student Activity Sheets 15A and 15B
- pencils or pens; scissors

Lesson Plan

1. PREPARE

Before class you should . . .
- review the lesson materials;

- consider which students you would like to have act as "artists" and "committee members."

Before class students should . . .
- complete Student Activity Sheet 15A as preparatory homework.

2. TEACH

Focus
- In a free-form manner, invite students to comment on the works of art they read about on Student Activity Sheet 15A.
- Ask them why people are making art that is inspired by the turn of the millennium.
- Ask them what criteria they would apply to such artworks to judge their worth as commemorations and celebrations of the turn of the millennium.

Guide
- Explain that students will simulate the role of an arts committee that is charged with choosing public art to commemorate the turn of the millennium in their own community.
- Distribute one copy of Student Activity Sheet 15B to each student. Assign volunteers the roles of artists and committee members.
- Follow the procedures on the activity sheet. As the committee members are meeting to develop the criteria, artists should meet to brainstorm ideas.
- When the artists receive the request forms from their committee, they should select the art ideas they have developed that conform

to the standards and complete the request forms.

- During this time, you should review the committee's work with the committee members.

Close

- Dissolve the student groupings. First, review the criteria created by the committee, and elicit artists' opinions about it.

- Review all of the works of art suggested. Point out the many different media that they include.

- Conclude by emphasizing the role of art in human affairs, and by focusing students' attention on the idea that millennial art can be a lasting testament to a very temporary event.

3. EVALUATE

- **Formal Evaluation** Collect and examine individual students' work on Student Activity Sheet 15A.

- **Informal Evaluation** Observe individual student's attitudes and contributions during the group work period.

- **Self-Evaluation** Have students consider these questions: What was the best thing I did while working with the group? and Which group member did I think made the best contribution, and how could I learn from his or her example?

4. EXTENSION AND ENRICHMENT

- Encourage students to actually create artwork inspired by the turn of the millennium in any medium they choose.

- Encourage students to participate in appropriate community events related to the turn of the millennium.

Teacher to Teacher   There will always be one student, or more, who would benefit greatly by doing artwork. You should go ahead and provide the materials and the encouragement for these students to explore their artistic nature, even if this isn't an "art class."

Journal Activities

You may wish to assign the self-evaluation questions as journal topics. As an alternative, challenge students to explore further this question: Why do people create art?

Art to Celebrate and Commemorate

People have always created works of art to celebrate and commemorate important events. Paintings, sculptures, plays, songs, dances—all the ways people express themselves artistically—have been used time and time again to mark great events.

The turn of the millennium will be no different. Around the world, people are planning, making, and putting the final touches on artwork to celebrate humanity's entrance into the third millennium.

Focus | Five works of art created to celebrate and commemorate the turn of the millennium are described below. As you read about them, consider your reaction to each one. Ask yourself: Would I be interested in viewing this art? Is this work of art an appropriate way to celebrate the turn of the millennium? Then answer the questions that follow. Use the back of your paper if you need more room to write.

Millennial Artwork: Five Examples

- An international group of photographers is planning to take pictures to record that last moment of the second millennium and the first moment of the third millennium. They then plan to arrange the photographs in various ways and present them in a traveling exhibit.

- An American company is planning to use lasers to project into the sky 2,000 colored stars (one for each year of the first two millennia).

- Many sculptors are taking inspiration from the turn of the millennium. One is making a house-sized globe from discarded items and titling the work *Millennium*.

- A poet has written a long work, titled "2000," that celebrates the improvement in life made over the last 1,000 years.

- Special coins are being designed by the mints of many countries to be issued at the turn of the millennium.

---

1. Which of these works of art would you most like to experience? Why?

2. Do any of these works of art strike you as particularly appropriate? In other words, do any seem to capture the true spirit of the turn of the millennium? Explain your answer.

3. Do any of these planned works of art seem somehow *inappropriate*? Do they seem unsuitable, irrelevant, or not right in some other way? Explain your answer.

4. Describe any additional millennial artwork you have seen or heard about.

Making Decisions About Public Art

Many of the thousands of pieces of art being created to celebrate and commemorate the turn of the millennium are *public* art. After all, the turn of the millennium is a very public event. What is public art? Public art is so-called because it is displayed in a public place. Any medium of art—painting, sculpture, dance—can be public art. For example, sculpture in a town square is public art. So is a dance performance to celebrate an anniversary.

Public art can be tricky, because not everyone agrees on what the best art is. In many communities, a special arts committee is given the responsibility for deciding what public art will be displayed.

Focus | Work with at least two other students to simulate the role of your local arts committee. Your task? To select the public art that will be displayed in your community to commemorate the turn of the millennium. To do this, you will establish standards for the artwork, and then invite local artists to submit ideas for works that meet these standards. You will then vote on which proposed piece of public art is the most appropriate one for your community. Take the following steps.

Step 1: Establish criteria

You need to establish the criteria, or standards, by which you will judge the proposed artworks. Working with the other arts committee members, answer these questions:

- What is the purpose of this piece of public art?

- Who will the audience for the art be?

- Where in your community will the art be presented to the public?

- Should the artwork be something that lasts a long time, like a sculpture? Or it should it be something temporary like a play, dance, or song? Why?

- Which medium do you prefer (painting, sculpture, something else)? Or would any medium be okay?

Now, use your answers to complete Part I of the form on the next page, which you will give to the artists.

(continued)

Making Decisions About Public Art *(continued)*

Millennium Art Idea Request Form

You are invited to submit your idea for a piece of public art to celebrate and commemorate the turn of the millennium in our community.

Part I. Your idea must meet the following standards:

The purpose of the art is to:

The audience of the art is:

The art will be presented to the community at:

The artwork you propose should last:

The medium you work in should be:

Part II. In the following space, describe your proposed piece of artwork. Also, supply a sketch if appropriate.

Step 2: Supply the form to the artists.

Photocopy and cut out the request form. Give it to student artists. They should complete Part II of the form, describing and sketching their ideas. They should then return the form to your committee.

Step 3: Reach a decision.

Meet with the other committee members to review the art ideas. Discuss each one, and vote to decide on the best idea. Explain how you came to your decision, and inform the class.

LESSON 16: **Happy New Millennium!**

Student Activity Sheet Disciplines and Levels

Student Activity Sheet	Discipline(s)	Level(s)
16A	social studies	A, B, C

Lesson Snapshot

Students study and respond to a map of the world with annotations that show how and where the turn of the millennium will be celebrated in many places.

Objectives

- Students will interpret a world map.
- Students will analyze the turn of the millennium as a worldwide event.
- Students will evaluate celebrations planned for the turn of the millennium.
- Students will apply the following critical thinking skills: interpretation, analysis, synthesis, and evaluation.

Class Time Required

- half of one class period

Materials Needed

- Student Activity Sheet 16A
- pencils or pens

Lesson Plan

1. PREPARE

Before class you should . . .

- review the lesson materials.

Before class students should . . .

- complete Student Activity Sheet 16A as preparatory homework.

2. TEACH

Focus

- Have students pull out their completed Student Activity Sheet 16A.

- Ask: What is the main idea of this map? Guide the class into a consensus.

Guide

- Ask students to share any comments they have about particular celebrations on the map.

- Go through the activity sheet questions with the class, using each as a springboard for a brief discussion.

- Focus students' attention on the nature of the places that people are traveling to celebrate the turn of the millennium.

Close

- Conclude by having students find the approximate location of their own community on the map and add a personalized annotation.

3. EVALUATE

- **Formal Evaluation** Collect and examine individual students' work on Student Activity Sheet 16A.

- **Informal Evaluation** Observe individual students' attitudes and contributions during the group discussion period.

- **Self-evaluation** Have students consider these questions: Why was it useful to have this information presented on a map? and How difficult was it for me to locate my own community on the map?

4. EXTENSION AND ENRICHMENT

- Encourage students to keep and annotate their maps with other important celebrations or events they read about.

Teacher to Teacher   This is largely a for-fun activity. Give students a chance to comment and laugh about some of the funnier things on the map, like the baby names.

Journal Activities

You may wish to assign the self-evaluation questions as journal topics. As an alternative, challenge students to explore further this question: Why is it important that I be familiar with the map of the world?

"People Want to Be Somewhere Special"

One hotel manager put it simply: "It's the millennium. People want to be somewhere special to ring in the next century."

Somewhere special, indeed! For more than a decade, people have been planning to be someplace extraordinary at midnight, December 31, 1999. (Never mind that the millennium doesn't technically turn until a year later!) From the North Pole to the South Pole—and some pretty interesting places in between—people have spent great amounts of money to be "somewhere special" at this very special moment in time.

Focus | The map on the following page highlights some special turn-of-the millennium celebrations. Study the map, and read the labels. Then respond to the questions that follow.

The North Pole Braving the cold, a few brave souls will mark the event at the "top of the world"—perhaps especially appropriate, for it is on the earth's axis.

The South Pole The south end of the earth's axis will also host a few brave—and cold—party-goers.

Stonehenge This mysterious site has already witnessed one turn of the millennium. Now people feel drawn to it for another.

The Pyramids The most famous and perhaps the most captivating structures in the world will serve as a gathering place for this special event.

The International Date Line A lucky few will be the first to see the new millennium in boats along the International Date Line.

Times Square In New York City, the most famous New Year's party in the world will be packed as never before.

At Sea Many cruise lines are running special cruises for people who want to ring in the millennium at sea.

Hotels and Restaurants Throughout the world, posh hotels and restaurants have been booked for years.

At Home Most people of the world will spend the night at home. For hundreds of millions who live under different calendars, the day has no special significance.

The Great Wall of China This monumental structure—4,000 miles long and more than 2,000 years old—has seen a lot of human history. It will witness the turn of the millennium along with the thousands of people from around the world who will gather there.

The Parthenon People will gather about the Parthenon in Athens, among the most beautiful buildings in the world and a symbol of human achievement.

The Vatican The center of the Catholic Church will hold special services.

Rio de Janeiro Famous for its celebration of other events, this cosmopolitan city is determined not to be outdone on this night of nights.

Sydney Beautiful Sydney harbor will be the site of a magnificent display of fireworks, a ship parade, and other shows.

Mexico City The largest city in the world will have one of the largest celebrations.

Hospitals Where will the first baby of the new millennium be born? Thousands of babies will be born near midnight. Experts say that many will be named "Milli," "Milliard," and even "Millennium."

(continued)

         Millennium: An Interdisciplinary Investigation

"People Want to Be Somewhere Special" *(continued)*

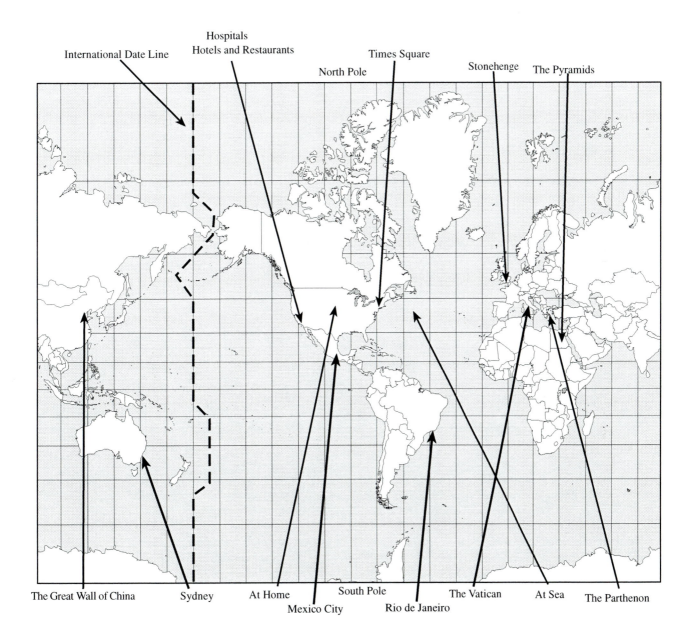

Hospitals
Hotels and Restaurants

International Date Line

North Pole

Times Square

Stonehenge   The Pyramids

The Great Wall of China   Sydney   At Home   South Pole   The Vatican   At Sea   The Parthenon

Mexico City   Rio de Janeiro

(continued)

"People Want to Be Somewhere Special" *(continued)*

1. How does the map show that the millennium is a worldwide event?

2. Do most of the places identified on the map have something in common? If so, what is it?

3. Which places on the map are sites of great natural beauty? Which are important human locations?

4. Do any of these places seem like an especially appropriate place for ringing in the new millennium? Why?

5. Do you find any of these places somehow *inappropriate*? Explain.

6. If you could be anywhere in the world at midnight, December 31, 1999, where would you choose to be? Why?

Unit IV

The Millennium That Will Be:

THE 21ST CENTURY AND BEYOND

LESSON 17: **What Year *Is* This?**

Student Activity Sheet Disciplines and Levels

Student Activity Sheet	Discipline(s)	Level(s)
17A	social studies; language arts	A, B, C
17B	social studies	A, B, C
17C	social studies; language arts	A, B, C

Lesson Snapshot

As preparatory homework, students read and respond individually to different ideas about what the first decade of the new millennium should be called. As an in-class activity, students work in groups to simulate a government policy meeting about naming the new decade. As a follow-up exercise, students read and analyze a humorous newspaper article about language difficulties posed by the turn of the millennium.

Objectives

- Students will analyze proposed names for a time period in historical and contemporary contexts.
- Students will simulate a governmental meeting.
- Students will apply the following critical thinking skills: interpretation, application, analysis, synthesis, and evaluation.

Time Required

- 1 class period

Materials Needed

- Student Activity Sheets 17A, 17B, and 17C
- pencils or pens

Lesson Plan

1. PREPARE

Before class you should . . .

- review the lesson materials;

- consider which students you would like to work together in small groups or as partners.

Before class students should . . .

- complete Student Activity Sheet 17A as preparatory homework.

2. TEACH

Focus

- Launch the lesson by writing "The Naughties" on the chalkboard and challenging volunteers to explain its significance.

- Once students have identified the naming of the new decade as the lesson focus, guide them into appreciating why such a name is important. Ask: Why is it important that the decade have a name? How will the name continue to affect people for many years?

- Next, guide students into expressing their opinions about what the decade should be named. Emphasize to them that they will live an important part of their lives during this decade, and so should be concerned about what it will be called. Lead a discussion on who, if anyone, students think should have the right and power to make such a decision.

Guide

- Explain to students that the National Institute of Standards and Technology (NIST) is a federal government agency in charge of setting standards for measurement. One measurement with which NIST is concerned is time. In response to repeated public queries, students should suppose that NIST has issued a recommendation for the name of the new decade. Explain that students will simulate the NIST meeting at which this recommendation is determined.

- Organize the class into several small groups. Each student should have his or her completed Student Activity Sheet 17A.

- Distribute one copy of Student Activity Sheet 17B to each group, and direct them to follow it as a group activity. You may wish to encourage each group to elect members to certain roles (a chairperson to run the meeting, a secretary to record members' ideas, etc.).

- Allow time for the groups to complete their tasks. As the students meet, circulate to keep them on track. Pay attention to particular students' attitudes and contributions. Challenge individual groups with objections to decade names they've thought of, or suggest additional names to stimulate their thinking. To ensure that students are working in a timely manner, you might wish to make periodic announcements that students should now move on to the next item on their agendas. For Item IV, the Press Release, you might remind students what a press release is and what questions it should answer (who, what, when, where, why).

Close

- Have a representative from each group read its press release. Tally and compare the groups' recommendations on the board.

- Conclude with a brief discussion about why people find it important to give names to the times of their lives. Ask: Why do people feel the need to name the times they live in?

- Distribute one copy of Student Activity Sheet 17C to each student as a homework assignment.

3. EVALUATE

- **Formal Evaluation** Collect and examine individual students' work on Student Activity Sheet 17A.

- **Informal Evaluation** Observe individual students' attitudes and contributions during the group work period.

- **Self-Evaluation** Have students consider these questions: What did I do especially well during my group's meeting? and What could I have done better?

4. EXTENSION AND ENRICHMENT

- Have students write summaries of the newspaper article in Student Activity Sheet 17C.

- Interested students can conduct research on the National Institute of Standards and Technology and share what they learn.

- Encourage students to conduct research to locate other essays and articles that address the issue of what the first decade of the new millennium should be called. Students may abstract the articles and share them with the class.

- Students should query other students and appropriate adults to find out what they think the first decade of the new millennium should be called, and why. Encourage students to structure these queries as a formal poll, and to present the results accordingly.

Teacher to Teacher This activity works especially well with heterogeneous, rather than homogenous, student groups. Heterogeneous groups give students a better chance to learn from each other's strengths and weaknesses.

Journal Activities

You may wish to assign the self-evaluation questions as journal topics. As an alternative, challenge students to explore further the closure question: Why do people feel the need to name the times they live in?

Name _____

Date _____

What Year *Is* This?
Student Activity Sheet 17A

Welcome to the Naughties

You may have been born in the eighties. Then came the nineties. But what will the first decade of the new millennium be called? The answer isn't as simple as you might think.

Focus | The following are suggestions for what to call the decade 2000–2009. Read each one and the reason people support the name. Supply a reason where none is given. As you work, ask yourself: What do I think the decade should be called?

What Should the Decade 2000–2009 Be Called?

Ten Ideas for the First Ten Years of the New Millennium

- **"the oughties"**
  because that's what the first decade of the twentieth century was called

- **the "00's"** (pronounced "the oh's")
  because it is logical and sounds nice

- **"the 2K's"**
  because K stands for *kilo,* or one thousand, in the metric system

- **"the zeroes"**

  because _____

- **"the singles"**

  because _____

- **"the naughties,"**
  because "a naught" means zero

- **"the zips"**

  because _____

- **"the OO's"** (pronounced the "oh-oh's")

  because _____

- **the "double O's"**

  because _____

- **"the M&M's"**
  because M stands for *milli,* which means one thousand, and

  because _____

As a young adult, you will shape the first decade of the new millennium. What do you think it should be called? Provide at least two reasons for your choice. Also, explain why you would object to the other names. Use the back of this paper to write your answers.

Name _____

Date _____

What Year *Is* This?
Student Activity Sheet 17B

A Challenge for NIST

Imagine you work for the federal government in Washington, D.C. Your job? You are a policy specialist for the National Institute of Standards and Technology (NIST).

NIST is the government agency in charge of setting standards for measurement. One of your agency's big concerns—especially with the turn of the millennium coming—is what to call the first decade of the new millennium. Although your agency does not have the power to declare the decade's official name, you are well aware that many individuals and reporters call frequently with the question, "What will the first decade of the new millennium be called?" You want to have an answer for them.

Focus | Today, you and your colleagues are meeting to review suggestions for the name and to choose one. The agenda of your meeting is presented here. Follow it carefully, and check off each item on the agenda as you complete it.

Agenda

Meeting of the New Millennium Committee

National Institute of Standards and Technology

The United States of America

Today's Date: _____

Item I. Identify possible names.

List below the names suggested for the first decade of the new millennium. (Use the essay "Welcome to the Naughties" and your own imagination for ideas.) List as many ideas as you can.

1.   6.

2.   7.

3.   8.

4.   9.

5.   10.

(continued)

A Challenge for NIST *(continued)*

Item II. Evaluate possible names.

On separate sheets of paper, make charts like the one below to help you evaluate each proposed name.

Proposed Name: _____	
Reasons For	**Reasons Against**
• _____ _____ _____ _____ _____ _____ _____ _____ _____ _____ _____ • _____ _____ _____ _____ _____ _____ _____ _____	• _____ _____ _____ _____ _____ _____ _____ _____ _____ _____ _____ • _____ _____ _____ _____ _____ _____ _____ _____

Item III. Make a recommendation.

As individuals, decide which name you think is the best choice. Then explain your choice to your colleagues. Through discussion, try to reach a consensus in which you and all of your colleagues agree on the name. If that is impossible, reach your final decision through a vote. Record the name you decided on below.

(continued)

Name _____

Date _____

What Year *Is* This?
Student Activity Sheet 17B

A Challenge for NIST *(continued)*

Item IV. Release and explain your recommendation.

As a group, draft a press release that explains and defends your recommendation.

Press Release

The New Millennium Names Committee

National Institute of Standards and Technology

The United States of America

Today's Date: _____

RE: THE NAME OF THE FIRST DECADE OF THE 21st CENTURY

_____   _____

_____   _____

_____   _____

_____   _____

_____   _____

_____   _____

_____   _____

_____   _____

_____   _____

_____   _____

_____   _____

_____   _____

A Speech Oddity

The new millennium raises important questions. Most are serious. What have we done right over the past 1,000 years? What have we done wrong? What will the next 1,000 years bring?

But many questions are just plain fun.

Focus | The following newspaper article tackles some of the fun questions raised by the turn of the millennium. Read the article, have a good laugh, and answer the questions that follow.

"Two thousand one" will be a speech oddity

For those of you who can't come up with enough of your own problems, here are some to add to your calendar. These are problems for the ages, ones never before encountered by humankind.

As we approach the turn of the century, America's general lack of math knowledge is rearing its ugly head. Problem No. 1 . . . is the general misapprehension that 2000 is the beginning of the 21st century.

It is not. It is the end of the 20th century. It could be the start of a new century only if the first year was called 0. It was not. It was 1.

Though turns of the century have come and gone, this one poses special problems. It's the first time in 1,000 years that we've changed the first number. It makes for years that don't sound like years. That's why you always say "the year 2000." The number by itself doesn't sound like a year. It sounds like a washing machine model with all kinds of features you'd never use.

We've never encountered this problem before. As you recall, 999 became 1000, though many folks found themselves saying "the year 1000," because 1000 didn't sound like a year. It sounded like a chariot style with all kinds of features you'd never use.

1000 was also the year of the big de-comma decision. Nobody seems to recall why . . . but the year was not denoted as 1,000.

(For the record, history also does not explain how things worked in the B.C. days, when years were counted backward. Remember when 454 faded into 453?)

In retrospect, the de-comma decision was a pivotal one that would have 1,000 years of consequences. It is probably why we say nineteen ninety-six, as opposed to one thousand, nine hundred ninety-six.

And that leads to the Real Problem.

Take this little quiz: Say out loud the name of the year after 1999.

If you are regular, you probably said "two thousand." If you said "twenty hundred," you show latent signs of journalism.

The quiz gets a little tougher here. Say the name of the year after 2000.

You probably said "two-thousand-one," though, following the lead of how we said years in the 20th century, you should have said "twenty-oh-one." But you didn't. You said "two-thousand-one" (or perhaps "two-thousand-and-one"). That decision was dictated by Hollywood. The 1968 movie *2001: A Space Odyssey* was pronounced "Two-thousand-one: *A Space Odyssey.*" It was not "Twenty-oh-one: *A Space Odyssey.*"

Now, say the name of the year after 2001. Though pollsters haven't checked on this, there is a good chance that a significant portion of you said "twenty-oh-two." Some might have even used the dreaded "twenty-ought-two," which sounds like a shotgun.

(continued)

Millennium: An Interdisciplinary Investigation

A Speech Oddity *(continued)*

But odds are good that 2002 will be two-thousand-two (the "and" is expected to last only one year), a result of the *Space Odyssey* deal. In fact, that pronunciation will probably carry us through two-thousand-nine.

The next problem crops up the day after Dec. 31, 2009. For reasons we don't know, two-thousand-nine will probably lead into twenty-ten. This may have something to do with our familiarity with twenty-twenty as a vision and TV show. Twenty-ten just sounds better to the American mouth than does two-thousand-ten.

Around 2010 also is when the Zager and Evans effect will kick in for those of us who had AM radios in 1969. That was the year in which the one-hit wonders reached the top of the charts with "In the Year 2525. . . ."

Zager (or was it Evans?) pronounced it "twenty-five-twenty-five," which fit the beat a whole lot better than "two thousand five-hundred and twenty-five" would have. . . .

1. What is the subject of the article?

2. What pun does the phrase "speech oddity" in the title make with something in the article?

3. (a) How does the writer think the year 2001 will be pronounced?

   (b) Why does he think people will pronounce it that way?

4. What problem does the writer say will crop up the day after December 31, 2009?

5. How would you describe the tone of this article? Is it serious, humorous, or something else? Or is it all three at the same time? Explain your answer.

LESSON 18: **Sending a Message to the Year 3000**

Student Activity Sheet Disciplines And Levels

Student Activity Sheet	Discipline(s)	Level(s)
18A	social studies; language arts	A, B, C

Lesson Snapshot

In this lesson, students plan to make a time capsule to be opened in the year 3000.

Objectives

- Students will explain the purpose of time capsules.
- Students will conceive a time capsule to be opened in the year 3000.
- Students will apply the following critical thinking skills: application, analysis, synthesis, and evaluation

Time Required

- 1 class period

Materials Needed

- Student Activity Sheet 18A
- pencils or pens

Lesson Plan

1. PREPARE

Before class you should . . .

- review the lesson materials;
- consider which students you would like to have work together in small groups.

2. TEACH

Focus

- Ask students what they would do if they had a time machine. After a few minutes, explain that one of the closest things we have to a time machine is a time capsule.

- Explain what a time capsule is, and inform students that in this lesson they will plan to make one.

Guide

- Organize the class into a few small working groups.

- Distribute one copy of Student Activity Sheet 18A to each student and direct students to complete it as a group activity. You may wish to encourage each group to elect members to certain roles (a chairperson to run the meeting, a secretary to record members' ideas, etc.).

- Allow time for the groups to complete their tasks. As the students meet, circulate to keep them on track. Pay attention to particular students' attitudes and contributions. Challenge individual groups with additional ideas for things to include in the time capsule. Tell them to stop after they complete Step 4.

Close

- Have a representative from each group describe the group's time capsule.

- Guide the class into reaching a consensus on the contents, container, and location of a time capsule.

- Conclude with a class activity in which students agree on the wording of a message to be included on the outside plaque of the time capsule (Step 5 of the activity sheet).

- Assign the second part of Step 5, the inside letter, as individual homework.

3. EVALUATE

- **Formal Evaluation** Collect and examine individual students' letters to the future.

- **Informal Evaluation** Observe individual students' attitudes and contributions during the group work period.
- **Self-Evaluation** Have students consider these questions: What did I do especially well during my group's meeting? and What could I have done better?

4. EXTENSION AND ENRICHMENT

- If possible, work with the school or another community organization to give students the chance to actually create a time capsule.

Teacher to Teacher   You can do this lesson in miniature by having students make a time capsule about their class (instead of the whole world) to be opened at the end of the school year or next year (not so far in the future).

Journal Activities

You may wish to assign the self-evaluation questions as journal topics. As an alternative, challenge students to explore further the closure question: Why do people feel the need to communicate with the people of the future through time capsules?

Making a Time Capsule

"Very cool!"

That's how one seventh-grader in Austin, Texas, described time capsules.

Time capsules *are* cool. After all, they're the closest things we have to time machines. A time capsule is simply a container with various items that is sealed for a long time, and then opened. Its purpose is to provide a record of a historical period for future generations. For example, in 1976, time capsules were buried across the country with instructions to be opened in 2076 or 2376 or another important date. The year 1976 was a special year—it was the bicentennial, or two hundredth birthday, of the United States. Americans created time capsules so that future Americans would know what America was like in 1976.

Focus | In this lesson, you'll have the opportunity to design a time capsule to show people at the next turn of the millennium what life is like at this turn of the millennium.

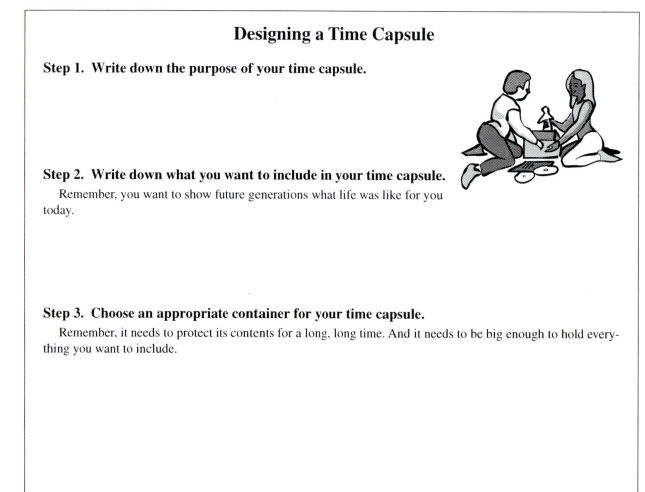

Designing a Time Capsule

Step 1. Write down the purpose of your time capsule.

Step 2. Write down what you want to include in your time capsule.

Remember, you want to show future generations what life was like for you today.

Step 3. Choose an appropriate container for your time capsule.

Remember, it needs to protect its contents for a long, long time. And it needs to be big enough to hold everything you want to include.

(continued)

Making a Time Capsule *(continued)*

Step 4. List possible sites for your time capsule.

Remember, it needs to be in a place where it won't be disturbed until it's supposed to be opened. But it also needs to be located in a place that can be easily found by the people of the future.

Step 5. Write a letter to the future.

You'll need to include two messages in your time capsule. One message will be on the outside of the container, explaining what the container is and when it should be opened. The second will be a letter inside the time capsule, which will convey any message you want to the people of A.D. 3000. Write the messages here.

Outside message:

Inside letter:

LESSON 19: **You and the Turn of the Millennium**

Student Activity Sheet Disciplines and Levels

Student Activity Sheet	Discipline(s)	Level(s)
19A	social studies; language arts	A, B, C

Lesson Snapshot

Students free-write about their own thoughts and feelings in response to this question: What does the turn of the millennium mean to you?

Objectives

- Students will compose their own thoughts about the turn of the millennium in the form of a personal essay.
- Students will apply the following critical thinking skills: interpretation, application, analysis, synthesis, and evaluation.

Time Required

- 1 class period

Materials Needed

- Student Activity Sheet 19A
- pencils or pens

Lesson Plan

1. PREPARE

Before class you should . . .

- review the lesson materials.

Before class students should . . .

- be thinking about what the turn of the millennium means to them personally.

2. TEACH

Focus

- Launch the lesson by writing "The Turn of the Millennium" on the chalkboard and inviting students to share the first thoughts that come to their minds.
- As students respond, focus the discussion on the salient, objective facts about the turn of the millennium.
- Then point out that, although the turn of the millennium is objectively a historical event with societal ramifications, it is ultimately a personal event that will be subjectively experienced by millions of individuals.

Guide

- Distribute one copy of Student Activity Sheet 19A to each student.
- As you pass out the activity sheets, explain to students that the sheet calls for them to share their reflections about what the turn of the millennium means to them personally.
- Emphasize that their responses will be confidential and will not be graded, and give them a generous amount of time to complete their work.

Close

- Collect the students' responses and write personalized replies.

3. EVALUATE

- Take this opportunity to informally evaluate students' thoughts and feelings about the turn of the millennium and develop appropriate responses.

Teacher to Teacher Here's a good opportunity for closure and reinforcement of understanding. If a student shows a lack of understanding, you can zero in on what needs to be done to help.

Name _____

Date _____

A Personal Reflection

Do you feel lucky to be alive when the millennium turns? Does it make you feel as if you are a part of history? Is it interesting to watch how other people respond to this historic occasion? Do you have your own hopes and dreams for your life during the third millennium?

This is your chance to share your own thoughts and feelings about what the turn of the millennium means to you, personally.

Focus

In the following space, write down whatever you care to about what the turn of the millennium means to you. You will not be graded on what you write, so do not worry about such things as spelling and punctuation. Instead, focus on your own thoughts and feelings. Answer this question: What does the turn of the millennium mean to you?